G. SCHIRMER OPERA ANTHOLOGY

ARIAS FOR SOPRANO

COMPLETE PACKAGE
with Diction Coach and Accompaniment CDs

Compiled and Edited by
Robert L. Larsen

Diction Coach includes International Phonetic Alphabet and diction lessons recorded by professional, native speaker coaches.

Accompaniment CDs were recorded by professional vocal coaches.

On the cover: "L'opéra de Paris" by Raoul Dufy
Used by permission of The Phillips Collection, Washington D.C.

ISBN 978-1-4803-2847-1

Complete Package released 2013

Copyright © 1991, 2008, 2011 by G. Schirmer, Inc. (ASCAP) New York, NY
International Copyright Secured. All Rights Reserved.
Warning: Unauthorized reproduction of this publication is
prohibited by Federal law and subject to criminal prosecution.

For all works contained herein:
Unauthorized copying, arranging, adapting, recording, Internet posting, public performance,
or other distribution of the recorded or printed content in this publication is an infringement of copyright.
Infringers are liable under the law.

G. SCHIRMER, Inc.

7777 W. BLUEMOUND RD. P.O. BOX 13819 MILWAUKEE, WI 53213

www.musicsalesclassical.com
www.halleonard.com

ROBERT L. LARSEN, editor and compiler of this anthology series, brings to the project experience from both professional opera and the academic realm. He is founder and artistic director of one of America's major opera festivals, the critically acclaimed Des Moines Metro Opera, and since the company's founding in 1973 has been conductor and stage director for all of its main stage productions. Since 1965 he has also been chairman of the department of music at Simpson College in Indianola, Iowa, and during his tenure the department has received national recognition and awards for its serious and extensive program of operatic training for undergraduates. Dr. Larsen holds a bachelor's degree from Simpson College, a master's degree in piano performance from the University of Michigan, and a doctoral degree in opera conducting from Indiana University. He is highly regarded as an opera coach and accompanist, and has assisted in the training of many artists with significant operatic careers.

The editor wishes to dedicate these volumes to the memory of Douglas Duncan, colleague and friend.

Editorial Advisor: Richard Walters
Aria Text Editor and Translator: Martha Gerhart
Assistant Editors: Patrick Hansen, William Casey
Music Engraving: Sangji International

On the cover: "L'opéra de Paris" by Raoul Dufy
Used by permission of The Phillips Collection, Washington, D.C.

CONTENTS

6 Notes and Translations

THE BALLAD OF BABY DOE
189 Willow Song
194 The Silver Aria

UN BALLO IN MASCHERA
85 Saper vorreste

LA BOHÈME
146 Mi chiamano Mimì
152 Quando men vo
156 Donde lieta

CARMEN
111 Je dis que rien ne m'épouvante

LES CONTES D'HOFFMANN
119 Elle a fui, la tourterelle!

DON GIOVANNI
50 Batti, batti, o bel Masetto
57 Vedrai, carino

FALSTAFF
140 Sul fil d'un soffio etesio

FAUST
88 Ah! Je ris de me voir (The Jewel Song)

FIDELIO
64 O wär' ich schon mit dir vereint

DER FREISCHÜTZ
71 Kommt ein schlanker Bursch gegangen

GIANNI SCHICCHI
166 O mio babbino caro

GIULIO CESARE
24 V'adoro, pupille

MADAMA BUTTERFLY
160 Un bel dì vedremo

MANON
124 Adieu, notre petite table

THE MEDIUM
176 The Black Swan
181 Monica's Waltz

LE NOZZE DI FIGARO
27 Porgi, amor
30 Dove sono i bei momenti
39 Deh vieni, non tardar

I PAGLIACCI
129 Stridono lassù

RIGOLETTO
79 Caro nome

ROMÉO ET JULIETTE
101 Ah! Je veux vivre

DER SCHAUSPIELDIREKTOR
44 Bester Jüngling

TARTUFFE
199 Fair Robin I love

TURANDOT
169 Signore, ascolta!
172 Tu che di gel sei cinta

DIE ZAUBERFLÖTE
61 Ach, ich fühl's

205 Diction Coach and IPA

265 Accompaniment CDs

FOREWORD

It has been a pleasure to reflect on the enormous repertory that the world of opera affords, and to choose from it a group of important and representative arias for soprano, mezzo-soprano, tenor, baritone, and bass to be included in these anthologies of opera arias.

In making these selections, I confess that I have not applied a constant criterion or standard, but rather have chosen to alter my perspective with each volume. All of these collections are intended to be of particular use to students and teachers of voice. Thus the soprano volume, for example, concentrates on lyric arias, rather than venturing very far into the rich material for coloratura, spinto, or dramatic voices.

The other volumes include the lyric arias most often sung by student voices, but also include other significant arias for a voice-type. For instance, I can't imagine a young baritone who would not be inspired by looking through the wonder of the Prologue from *I Pagliacci* within the confines of his practice room, or a tenor who doesn't anticipate with excitement the day when "Che gelida manina" may fit his voice like a glove. On the other hand, I have omitted some important repertory, such as many of the great Verdi baritone arias, because they are widely available, and are certainly the province of only the most experienced performer. Instead, I have chosen pieces of value not previously found in such collections, including arias in English for each voice-type.

Each aria has been painstakingly researched in preparing these new editions, creating what I believe will be an eminently credible and useful source for this music. There are countless incidents where notes or words have been corrected to create a more substantiated presentation than in previous editions. Throughout the collections, one will find many spots where traditional cadenzas are recommended. Appropriate appoggiaturas, as defined by conservative application of tradition, are indicated as well. There are instances where an entirely revised piano reduction, more representative of the full score, has been created.

These anthologies are for all of us who must remain students of our art throughout our lifetimes. I'm a vocal coach and opera conductor who believes firmly in exposing the gifted performer to the firmament, being sure that he or she understands that each star must be attained at its own special time, to be plucked and polished again and again throughout a musical career. Among these arias may be the first one ever studied, but if it's by someone destined to be a real singer, it will remain in mind and heart forever.

Robert L. Larsen
March, 1991

NOTES and TRANSLATIONS

Translator's Note

My aim in providing these "literal" translations was to give accurate line-by-line translations, as opposed to word-by-word translations. At the same time, the goal was to translate a true sense of the thought of each word or phrase.

In this format, therefore, the words on each line of original language text correspond to the words on each line of translation. Whenever, for contextual and idiomatic reasons, a line-by-line format into English is not possible, the printing is indented. In such cases, the whole idea of the indented foreign-language text segment corresponds to the whole idea of the indented English translation segment.

There are many antiquated and poetic word forms in opera texts which appear in various usages. In editing the aria texts various punctuation was discovered in various sources. When challenged by discrepancies, I have made justifiable choices for this edition. In some cases the punctuation has been modernized in the interest of clarity or consistency.

M. G.

NOTES and TRANSLATIONS

The arias are presented chronologically by year of first performance.

GUILIO CESARE
(Julius Caesar)
1724
music by George Frideric Handel
libretto by Nicola Francesco Haym (after history and legend)

V'adoro, pupille

from Act II
setting: Egypt, 48 B.C.; Cleopatra's palace
character: Cleopatra

As part of her plan to captivate Caesar, Cleopatra arranges a tableau representing Mount Parnassus and appears as Virtue surrounded by the Muses.

V'adoro, pupille,	*I adore you, eyes,*
saette d'amore;	*darts of love;*
le vostre faville	*your sparks*
son grate nel sen.	*are welcome in my breast.*
Pietose vi brama	*My sad heart,*
il mesto mio core,	*which calls you its dearly beloved*
ch'ogn'ora vi chiama	*in every hour, longs for you*
l'amato suo ben.	*to be compassionate.*

LE NOZZE DI FIGARO
(The Marriage of Figaro)
1786
music by Wolfgang Amadeus Mozart
libretto by Lorenzo da Ponte (after *La Folle Journée, ou Le Mariage de Figaro*, a comedy by Pierre Augustin Caron de Beaumarchais)

Porgi, amor

from Act II
setting: near Seville, the 17th century; the palace of Count Almaviva; the Countess' apartment
character: Countess Almaviva

The Countess Almaviva, still young and beautiful, knows that her husband has developed a roving eye for other ladies of the castle, and is shamed and hurt by his neglect and deceit. Alone in her bed chamber as the act opens, she prays to the god of love to assist her in her hour of need.

Porgi, amor,	*Grant, Love,*
qualche ristoro	*some relief*
al mio duolo,	*to my sorrow,*
a' miei sospir!	*to my sighing!*
O mi rendi	*Either give me back*
il mio tesoro,	*my beloved,*
o mi lascia almen	*or just let me*
morir!	*die!*

The historical notes and synopses in this section are by the editor; translations are by Martha Gerhart.

Dove sono i bei momenti

from Act III
setting: near Seville, the 17th century; a hall in the palace of Count Almaviva
character: Countess Almaviva

An elaborate plot has been laid by the Countess, with the aid of Susanna and Figaro, to expose her husband's infidelty. In *recitativo accompagnato*, Countess Almaviva muses on the fact that she has even had to enlist the aid of her chamber maid in an attempt to stop the Count's flirtations. In the aria which follows she ponders her future, and yearns for the return of her husband's affection.

E Susanna non vien!	And Susanna doesn't arrive!
Sono ansiosa di saper come il Conte	I am anxious to know how the Count
accolse la proposta.	reacted to the proposal.
Alquanto ardito il progetto mi par,	The plan seems to me rather bold,
e ad uno sposo sì vivace	especially with a husband so high-strung
e geloso!	and jealous!
Ma che mal c'è?	But what harm is there
cangiando i miei vestiti	in changing my clothes
con quelli di Susanna,	with those of Susanna,
e i suoi co' miei	and hers with mine,
al favor della notte.	under the cover of night?
Oh cielo!	Oh heaven!
A qual umil stato fatale	To what an unfortunate state of humility
io son ridotta da un consorte crudel!	I have been reduced by a cruel husband
che dopo avermi con un misto inaudito	who—with an incredible mixture
d'infedeltà, di gelosia, di sdegno!	of infidelity, jealousy, and disdain—
prima amata,	after having first loved me,
indi offesa,	having then offended me,
e alfin tradita,	and having finally betrayed me,
fammi or cercar	causes me now to seek
da una mia serva aita!	help from one of my servants!
Dove sono i bei momenti	Where are the beautiful moments
di dolcezza e di piacer?	of sweetness and of pleasure?
Dove andaro i giuramenti	Where did the promises
di quel labbro menzogner?	of those lying lips go?
Perchè mai, se in pianti e in pene	Why ever, if in tears and in suffering
per me tutto si cangiò,	everything has changed for me,
la memoria di quel bene	has the memory of that dear one
dal mio sen non trapassò?	not left my breast?
Ah! se almen la mia costanza	Ah, if only my constancy
nel languire amando ognor	while languishing, always loving,
mi portasse una speranza	may bring me a hope
di cangiar l'ingrato cor.	of changing his ungrateful heart.

Deh vieni, non tardar

from Act IV
setting: near Seville, the 17th century; the palace garden of Count Almaviva; night
character: Susanna

The Countess is disguised as her chamber maid, Susanna, in order to trick her husband, the Count, who thinks he is meeting Susanna herself. Susanna, married only hours before to Figaro, appears disguised as her mistress and sings this recitative and arietta, which seems to be the girl's enchanting imitation of the Countess' restrained and elegant way of seeing, speaking, and singing. She is aware that her husband is listening.

Giunse alfin il momento
   che godrò senza affanno
   in braccio all'idol mio.
Timide cure!
uscite dal mio petto;
a turbar non venite
il mio diletto!
Oh come par che
all'amoroso foco
l'amenità del loco,
la terra e il ciel
risponda,
come la notte
i furti miei seconda!
	The moment which I will enjoy
	   without anxiety, in the arms of
	   my idol, has finally arrived.
	Timid feelings,
	leave my breast;
	don't come to disturb
	my pleasure!
	Oh, how it seems that
	to amorous passion
	the pleasantness of the place,
	the earth, and the sky
	respond,
	as the darkness
	favors my connivings!

Deh vieni,
non tardar, o gioja bella.
Vieni ove amore
per goder t'appella
finchè non splende in ciel
   notturna face–
finchè l'aria è ancor bruna,
e il mondo tace.
Qui mormora il ruscel,
qui scherza l'aura,
   che col dolce susurro
   il cor ristaura,
qui ridono i fioretti
e l'erba è fresca.
Ai piaceri d'amor
qui tutto adesca.
Vieni, ben mio,
tra queste piante ascose!
Ti vo' la fronte incoronar
di rose.
	Please come;
	don't delay, oh beautiful joy.
	Come to where love
	calls you to enjoy yourself
	until the nocturnal torch doesn't
	   shine in the sky anymore—
	until it's dark again,
	and the world is still.
	Here the stream murmurs;
	here the breeze, which revives
	   the heart with its gentle
	   rustling, plays.
	Here little flowers are laughing,
	and the grass is fresh.
	To the pleasures of love
	everything here is enticing.
	Come, my dear,
	among these sheltering trees!
	I want to crown your head
	with roses.

DER SCHAUSPIELDIREKTOR

(The Impresario)
1786
music by Wolfgang Amadeus Mozart
libretto by Gottlieb Stephanie, the younger

Bester Jüngling

in one act
setting: the office of an opera impresario, the 18th century
character: Fräulein Silberklang

This *singspiel* was written for festivities at Vienna's Schönbrunn Palace, at which an *opera seria* by Salieri was also premiered. With this aria a young soubrette successfully auditions for the weary and beleagured impresario of an opera company.

Bester Jüngling, mit Entzükken nehm' ich deine Liebe an, da in deinen holden Blikken ich mein Glück entdekken kann.	*Good young man, with enchantment* *I accept your love,* *for in your pleasing glances* *I can discover my happiness.*
Aber ach, wenn düst'res Leiden unsrer Liebe folgen soll, lohnen dies der Liebe Freuden? Jüngling, das bedenke wohl!	*But, ah, if sad suffering* *should ensue from our love,* *is that worth the joys of love?* *Young man, consider that carefully!*
Nichts ist mir so wert und teuer, als dein Herz und deine Hand. Voll vom reinsten Liebesfeuer geb' ich dir mein Herz zum Pfand.	*Nothing is as worthy and precious to me* *as your heart and your hand.* *Full of the purest ardor of love* *I give you my heart in pledge.*

DON GIOVANNI

1787
music by Wolfgang Amadeus Mozart
libretto by Lorenzo da Ponte (after Giovanni Bertati's libretto for Giuseppe Gazzaniga's *Il convitato di pietra;* also after the Don Juan legends)

Batti, batti, o bel Masetto

from Act I, scene 4
setting: Seville, the 17th century; the garden of Don Giovanni's palace; late afternoon
character: Zerlina

Zerlina and Masetto, a peasant couple, are about to be married. The festivities have begun when Giovanni happens on the scene and becomes enamored of the charming Zerlina. He tries to lead her to his castle and almost succeeds. In this aria a contrite Zerlina teases and kisses her offended fiancé into good humor again.

Ma se colpa io non ho!	*But I'm not guilty!*
Ma se da lui ingannata rimasi...	*But I was tricked by him...*
E poi che temi?	*And so what are you afraid of?*
Tranquillati, mia vita:	*Be assured, love of my life:*
non mi toccò la punta delle dita.	*he didn't touch the tip of my finger.*
Non me lo credi?	*Don't you believe me?*
Ingrato!	*Ungrateful!*
Vien qui, sfogati, ammazzami—	*Come here. Vent your anger; kill me—*
fa' tutto di me quel che ti piace;	*do anything you please to me.*
ma poi, Masetto mio,	*But afterwards, my Masetto,*
fa' pace.	*make peace.*
Batti, o bel Masetto,	*Hit, oh handsome Masetto,*
la tua povera Zerlina.	*your poor Zerlina.*
Starò qui come agnellina	*Like a little lamb*
le tue botte ad aspettar.	* I'll await your blows.*
Lascerò straziarmi il crine,	*I'll let my hair be pulled out.*
lascerò cavarmi gli occhi,	*I'll let my eyes be scratched out.*
e le care tue manine lieta poi	*And then, happy, I will be able to kiss*
saprò baciar.	* your dear beloved hands.*
Ah, lo vedo, non hai core:	*Ah, I see it: you don't have courage!*
Pace, o vita mia;	*Peace, oh love of my life!*
in contenti ed allegria	*In contentment and good cheer*
notte e dì vogliam passar,	*let's enjoy passing the nights and days.*
sì sì...	*Yes, yes...*

Vedrai, carino

from Act II, scene 1
setting: Seville, the 17th century; a street in front of the house where Donna Elvira is staying; night
character: Zerlina

Giovanni, disguised as his servant Leporello, viciously beats the peasant lad Masetto. When Zerlina, the boy's bride-to-be, comes on the scene she sympathizes with Masetto, assuring him that love can heal all wounds.

Vedrai, carino,	*You will see, dearest,*
se sei buonino,	*if you are good,*
che bel rimedio	*what fine medicine*
ti voglio dar.	*I want to give you.*
E naturale,	*It's natural.*
non da disgusto,	*It's not unpleasant;*
e lo speziale	*and the pharmacist*
non lo sa far,	*doesn't know how to make it—*
no, non lo sa far.	*no, he doesn't know how to make it.*

È un certo balsamo	*It's a certain balm*
che porto addosso.	*that I carry with me.*
Dare te'l posso,	*I can give it to you,*
se'l vuoi provar.	*if you want to try it.*
Saper vorresti	*Would you like to know*
dove mi sta?	*where I have it?*
Sentilo battere,	*Feel it beat;*
toccami qua.	*touch me here.*

DIE ZAUBERFLÖTE

(The Magic Flute)
1791
music by Wolfgang Amadeus Mozart
libretto by Emanuel Schikaneder (loosely based on a fairy tale by Wieland)

Ach, ich fühl's

from Act II, scene 4
setting: Legendary; the inner shrine of the sacred brotherhood
character: Pamina

Pamina is despondent because her beloved, the Prince Tamino, no longer speaks to her and seems to shun her presence. She does not know that he has sworn a vow of silence as part of the ceremony of initiation to Sarastro's brotherhood.

Ach, ich fühl's, es ist verschwunden,	*Ah, I feel it; it has vanished—*
ewig hin der Liebe Glück!	*forever gone, the happiness of love!*
Nimmer kommt ihr, Wonnestunden,	*Never will you, blissful hours,*
meinem Herzen mehr zurück.	*come back again to my heart.*
Sieh, Tamino, diese Tränen fließen,	*See, Tamino, these tears flow,*
Trauter, dir allein.	*beloved one, for you alone.*
Fühlst du nicht der Liebe Sehnen,	*If you do not feel the longing of love,*
so wird Ruh im Tode sein.	*then peace will come to be in death.*

FIDELIO

1805
music by Ludwig van Beethoven
libretto by Josef Sonnleithner; revised by Stephan von Breuning and Georg Friedrich Treitschke (after Jean Nicolas Bouilly's play *Léonore, ou L'Amour Conjugal*)

O wär' ich schon mit dir vereint

from Act I
setting: Seville, the 18th century; the courtyard of the prison fortress
character: Marzelline

Marzelline is the daughter of Rocco, the jailer. Jaquino, her father's assistant, thought that he and Marzelline were destined to wed until the handsome Fidelio joined the work force at the prison. Marzelline sings of her ardent longing for Fidelio, not knowing that he is really the disguised Leonore, wife of Florestan, a prisoner.

O wär' ich schon mit dir vereint,	*Oh, were I already united with you,*
und dürfte Mann dich nennen!	*and could call you husband!*
Ein Mädchen darf ja, was es meint,	*A young girl must, of course, admit to*
zur Hälfte nur bekennen!	*only half of what she is thinking!*
Doch wenn ich nicht erröthen muß	*But, when I won't have to blush*
ob einem warmen Herzenskuß,	*because of a warm, caressing kiss...*
wenn nichts uns stört auf Erden...	*when nothing on earth will disturb us...*
Die Hoffnung schon erfüllt die Brust	*Hope already fills my breast*
mit unaussprechlich süßer Lust;	*with unspeakably sweet pleasure;*
wie glücklich will ich werden!	*how happy I will be!*

In Ruhe stiller Häuslichkeit	*In the quiet of peaceful domesticity*
erwach' ich jeden Morgen.	*I will wake up each morning.*
Wir grüßen uns mit Zärtlichkeit;	*We will greet each other with tenderness;*
der Fleiss verscheucht die Sorgen.	*diligent work will drive away anxieties.*
Und ist die Arbeit abgethan,	*And when the work is put aside,*
dann schleicht die holde Nacht heran;	*then lovely night will descend;*
dann ruh'n wir von Beschwerden.	*then we will rest from cares.*
Wie will ich glücklich werden!	*How happy I will be!*

DER FREISCHÜTZ

(The Free-shooter)
1821
music by Carl Maria von Weber
libretto by Johann Friedrich Kind (after a story by Johann August Apel and Friedrich Laun and Gothic legend)

Kommt ein schlanker Bursch gegangen

from Act II, scene 1
setting: Mythical, ancient Germany; the home of Cuno, the chief forester (formerly the royal hunting lodge)
character: Ännchen

If Max is successful in a shooting contest he can win the title of chief forester and the right to marry his beloved Agathe, the daughter of Cuno. It is the eve of the big day, and Agathe is sad and nervous. Her spirited cousin Ännchen succeeds in cheering her up with a song.

Kommt ein schlanker Bursch gegangen,	*Should a slender fellow come along,*
blond von Locken oder braun,	*blond haired or dark,*
hell von Aug' und roth von Wangen,	*bright eyed and rosy cheeked,*
ei, nach dem kann man wohl schau'n!	*indeed, one may certainly ogle him!*
Zwar schlägt man das Aug' auf's Mieder	*To be sure, one lowers her eyes to her bodice,*
nach verschämter Mädchen Art;	*in the manner of bashful young girls;*
doch verstohlen hebt man's wieder,	*but one raises them again furtively*
wenn's das Herrchen nicht gewahrt.	*when the young gentleman isn't watching.*
Sollten ja sich Blicke finden,	*Should they even exchange glances,*
nun, was hat das auch für Noth?	*now what danger is there in that?*
Man wird drum nicht gleich erblinden,	*One will not become blind from it,*
wird man auch ein wenig roth.	*though one will become a little flushed.*
Blickchen hin und Blick herüber,	*A little glance here and a glance there,*
bis der Mund sich auch was traut.	*until the mouth also ventures something.*
Er seufzt: Schönste!	*He sighs, "Most beautiful one!"*
Sie spricht: Lieber!	*She says, "Dearest!"*
Bald heißt's Bräutigam und Braut.	*Soon they are bridegroom and bride.*
Immer näher, liebe Leutchen,	*Come closer still, dear folks—*
wollt ihr mich im Kranze seh'n?	*do you want to see me in a bridal wreath?*
Gelt! das ist ein nettes Bräutchen,	*"Hey, that's a pretty little bride,*
und der Bursch nicht minder schön!	*and the fellow no less attractive!"*

RIGOLETTO

1851
music by Giuseppe Verdi
libretto by Francesco Maria Piave (after Victor Hugo's drama *Le Roi s'Amuse*)

Caro nome

from Act II when played in four acts; Act I, scene 2 when played in three acts
setting: Mantua, the 16th century; a deserted street outside Rigoletto's house; night
character: Gilda

The hunchback Rigoletto is a jester at court. His wife is dead, and he has always concealed his lovely daughter, Gilda, from the world. At mass she has met a handsome young man who makes his way into their walled garden and declares his love. She muses on his name, Gualtier Maldè, not suspecting that he is really the Duke of Mantua, Rigoletto's employer, in search of adventure.

Gualtier Maldè!	"Gualtier Maldè,"
nome di lui sì amato,	name of him so much loved,
ti scolpisci	you engrave yourself
nel core innamorato!	in my enamored heart!

Caro nome che il mio cor
   festi primo palpitar,
le delizie dell'amor
   mi dêi sempre rammentar!
Col pensier il mio desir
a te sempre volerà,
e fin l'ultimo sospir,
caro nome, tuo sarà.
Il mio desir a te
   ognora volerà!

Dear name, which first made
   my heart throb,
you must always recall to me
   the delights of love!
In my thoughts, my desire
will always fly to you;
and even my last breath,
dear name, will be yours.
My desire will evermore
   fly to you!

UN BALLO IN MASCHERA
(A Masked Ball)
1859
music by Giuseppe Verdi
libretto by Antonio Somma (after Eugène Scribe's libretto for Daniel-François Auber's *Gustave III, ou Le Bal Masqué*)

Saper vorreste

from Act II, scene 2
setting: Stockholm, 1792 (or Boston, depending on the version played); a state ballroom
character: Oscar

Oscar is the faithful page of Riccardo, King of Sweden or Governor of Boston, depending upon the version performed. The page is asked by Renato, secretary to Riccardo and secretly intent on the ruler's assassination, the nature of Riccardo's disguise at the masked ball they are attending. Oscar playfully refuses to divulge the information.

Saper vorreste di che si veste,
quando l'è cosa ch'ei vuol nascosa.
Oscar lo sa, ma nol dirà.
Tra la la…

You would like to know how he is costumed,
when that is the thing he wants concealed.
Oscar knows it, but will not say it.
Tra la la…

Pieno d'amor mi balza il cor,
ma pur discreto serba il segreto.
Nol rapirà grado o beltà.
Tra la la…

Full of love my heart is throbbing
but yet, discreetly, is keeping the secret.
Neither rank nor beauty will carry it away.
Tra la la…

FAUST
1859
music by Charles Gounod
libretto by Jules Barbier and Michel Carré (after the drama by Johann Wolfgang von Goethe)

Ah! Je ris de me voir
(The Jewel Song)

from Act III when played in five acts; Act II when played in four acts
setting: a German village, the 16th century; Marguerite's garden
character: Marguerite

Faust, an aging philosopher who has struck a bargain with the devil to regain his youth, is entranced by a lovely young maiden, Marguerite. One day Marguerite finds on her doorstep a beautiful casket which she soon discovers contains magnificent jewels, and which she later learns is a gift from Faust.

Que vois-je là?	What do I see there?
D'où ce riche coffret peut-il venir?	Where can that splendid little chest come from?
Je n'ose y toucher, et pourtant…	I dare not touch it, and yet…
Voici la clef, je crois!	Here is the key, I believe!
Si je l'ouvrais!	What if I should open it?
Ma main tremble! Pourquoi?	My hand is trembling! Why?
Je ne fais, en l'ouvrant, rien de mal, je suppose!	I'm not doing anything wrong by opening it, I guess!
Ô Dieu! que de bijoux!	Oh God—what jewels!
Est-ce un rêve charmant qui m'éblouit, ou si je veille?	Is this a pleasant dream that is dazing me? Or, what if I am awake?
Mes yeux n'ont jamais vu de richesse pareille!	My eyes have never seen such opulence!
Si j'osais seulement me parer un moment de ces pendants d'oreille!	If only I dared to adorn myself for a moment with these earrings!
Ah! Voici justement, au fond de la cassette: un miroir!	Ah! Here is just what I need, at the bottom of the box: a mirror!
Comment n'être pas coquette?	How not to be coquettish?
Ah! Je ris de me voir si belle en ce miroir!	Ah! I'm smiling, seeing myself so beautiful in this mirror!
Est-ce toi, Marguerite?	Is it you, Marguerite?
Réponds-moi; réponds vite!	Answer me; answer quickly!
Non! ce n'est plus toi!	No, it's no longer you!
Ce n'est plus ton visage; c'est la fille d'un roi qu'on salue au passage!	It's no longer your face; it's the daughter of a king to whom people bow as she passes!
Ah, s'il était ici!	Ah, if he were here!
S'il me voyait ainsi!	If he could see me like this!
Comme une demoiselle il me trouverait belle!	Like a lady of gentility he would find me beautiful!
Achevons la métamorphose.	Let's complete the transformation.
Il me tarde encor d'essayer le bracelet et le collier!	I'm most eager to try the bracelet and the necklace!
Dieu! c'est comme une main, qui sur mon bras se pose!	God! It's like a hand that sets itself upon my arm!
Ah!…	Ah!…

ROMÉO ET JULIETTE
(Romeo and Juliet)
1867
music by Charles Gounod
libretto by Jules Barbier and Michel Carré (after the tragedy by William Shakespeare)

Ah! Je veux vivre
(Juliette's Waltz Song)

from Act I
setting: Verona, the 14th century; the ballroom of the Capulet palace
character: Juliette

The Capulets are celebrating Juliette Capulet's birthday with a masked ball, unaware that the despised Montagues, including the handsome Roméo, are among them. Roméo is enchanted when Juliette, whom he has never seen before, sings with childlike exuberance of her sheer joy in being alive on this wonderful night.

Ah! Je veux vivre dans le rêve qui m'enivre ce jour encor! Douce flamme, je te garde dans mon âme comme un trésor!	Ah! I want to live in the dream which still intoxicates me on this day! Gentle flame, I keep you in my soul as a treasure!
Cette ivresse de jeunesse ne dure, hélas! qu'un jour. Puis vient l'heure où l'on pleure; le cœur cède à l'amour, et le bonheur fuit sans retour!	This rapture of youth only lasts, alas, for a day. After that comes the hour when one weeps; the heart gives way to love, and happiness flies away, never to return!
Ah! Je veux vivre dans le rêve qui m'enivre longtemps encor! Loin de l'hiver morose laisse-moi sommeiller et respirer la rose avant de l'effeuiller.	Ah! I want to live in the dream, which intoxicates me, for a long time still! Far from gloomy winter let me slumber and inhale the rose before shedding it of its petals.
Ah! Douce flamme, reste dans mon âme comme un doux trésor longtemps encor!	Ah! Gentle flame, stay in my soul as a sweet treasure for a long time still!

CARMEN

1875
music by Georges Bizet
libretto by Henri Meilhac and Ludovic Halévy (after the novel by Prosper Mérimée)

Je dis que rien ne m'épouvante

from Act III
setting: in the mountains near the Spanish border, c. 1820; night
character: Micaëla

Seduced by the gypsy girl Carmen, Don José has abandoned his post with the dragoons in Seville and has joined the gypsy smuggling operation. Led by a mountain guide, his childhood sweetheart, Micaëla, searches for him to tell him that his dying mother wants to see him one last time. Micaëla prays for the strength to brave the wilderness and face her beloved José and the woman who has bewitched him.

C'est des contrebandiers le refuge ordinaire. Il est ici; je le verrai! Et le devoir que m'imposa sa mère— sans trembler je l'accomplirai.	This is the usual hideout of the smugglers. He is here; I will see him! And the task which his mother entrusted to me— without trembling, I will accomplish it.
Je dis que rien ne m'épouvante. Je dis, hélas! que je réponds de moi; mais j'ai beau faire la vaillante… au fond du cœur je meurs d'effroi!	I say that nothing frightens me. I say, alas, that I can fend for myself; but I'm trying in vain to be brave… in the depth of my heart I'm dying of anxiety!
Seule en ce lieu sauvage— toute seule j'ai peur, mais j'ai tort d'avoir peur. Vous me donnerez du courage; vous me protégerez, Seigneur!	Alone in this wild place— all alone—I'm afraid, but I'm wrong to be afraid. You will give me courage; you will protect me, Lord!

Je vais voir de près cette femme	I am going to see close-up that woman
dont les artifices maudits ont fini	whose cursed tricks succeeded
par faire un infâme	in making a criminal
de celui que j'aimais jadis!	of him whom I loved long ago!
Elle est dangereuse…	She is dangerous…
elle est belle!	she is beautiful!
Mais je ne veux pas avoir peur!	But I don't want to be afraid!
Non, non, je ne veux pas avoir peur!	No, no, I don't want to be afraid!
Je parlerai haut devant elle…	I will speak proudly in front of her…
Ah! Seigneur, vous me protégerez!	Ah, Lord, you will protect me!
Protégez-moi! Ô Seigneur!	Protect me, oh Lord!
Donnez-moi du courage!	Give me courage!
Protégez-moi, Seigneur!	Protect me, Lord!

LES CONTES D'HOFFMANN
(The Tales of Hoffmann)
1880
music by Jacques Offenbach
libretto by Jules Barbier and Michel Carré (after stories of E. T. A. Hoffmann)

The opera was incomplete at the time of Offenbach's death in 1880; completed, edited and orchestrated by Ernest Guiraud and others.

Elle a fui, la tourterelle!

from Act III or Act II, depending on the order played
setting: Munich, the 19th century; a parlor in the home of Crespel
character: Antonia

One of the acts of this fantastic opera, based on stories of the German author and composer E. T. A. Hoffmann, is about Antonia, the daughter of Crespel and a deceased opera singer whose portrait dominates the scene. The girl is forbidden to sing because of the precarious nature of her health, but she gives voice to this plaintive melody, lamenting the absence of her beloved, the poet Hoffmann.

Elle a fui, la tourterelle!	She has fled—the turtle dove!
Ah! souvenir trop doux!	Ah, memory too sweet!
Image trop cruelle!	Image too bitter!
Hélas! à mes genoux	Alas, at my knees
je l'entends, je le vois!	I hear him, I see him!
Elle a fui, la tourterelle.	She has fled—the turtle dove.
Elle a fui loin de toi;	She has fled far from you;
mais elle est toujours fidèle	But she is forever faithful
et te garde sa foi.	and keeps her promise to you.
Mon bien-aimé, ma voix t'appelle.	My beloved, my voice calls to you.
Oui, tout mon cœur est à toi.	Yes, all my heart is yours.
Chère fleur qui viens d'éclore,	Precious flower which has just bloomed,
par pitié, réponds-moi!	for pity's sake answer me,
toi qui sais s'il m'aime encore,	you who knows if he still loves me,
s'il me garde sa foi!	if he keeps his promise to me!
Mon bien-aimé, ma voix t'implore.	My beloved, my voice implores you.
Ah! que ton cœur vienne à moi.	Ah, may your heart come to me.

MANON
1884
music by Jules Massenet
libretto by Henri Meilhac and Philippe Gille (after the novel *L'Histoire du Chevalier des Grieux et de Manon Lescaut* by Abbé Prévost)

Adieu, notre petite table

from Act II
setting: Paris, 1721; the apartment of Des Grieux and Manon in the Rue Vivienne
character: Manon

The young Manon was on the way to a convent school when she met and eloped to Paris with the Chevalier des Grieux. Now, unbeknownst to her lover, Manon is being courted by a man who promises her wealth befitting her beauty. Tormented by her own frailty but entranced by visions of a glamorous life, she bids farewell to the little table that symbolizes the happiness that she and Des Grieux knew together.

Allons! il le faut!	Come on, it is necessary,
pour lui même!	for his own sake!
Mon pauvre chevalier!	My poor chevalier!
Oh! oui, c'est lui que j'aime!	Oh yes, it is he whom I love!
Et pourtant, j'hésite aujourd'hui!	And yet, today I hesitate!
Non, je ne suis plus digne de lui!	No, I am no longer worthy of him!
J'entends cette voix qui m'entraîne	I hear that voice which transports me
contre ma volonté:	against my will:
«Manon! Manon, tu seras reine—	"Manon! Manon, you will be queen—
reine par la beauté!»	queen in the name of beauty!"
Je ne suis que faiblesse	I am nothing but weakness
et que de fragilité!	and fragility!
Ah! malgré moi	Ah, without wanting to,
je sens couler mes larmes	I feel my tears flowing
devant ces rêves effacés!	in the face of those destroyed dreams!
L'avenir aura-t-il les charmes	Will the future have the charms
de ces beaux jours déjà passés?	of those beautiful days already past?
Adieu, notre petite table,	Farewell, our little table
qui nous réunit si souvent!	which brought us together so often!
Adieu, notre petite table,	Farewell, our little table
si grande pour nous cependant!	so grand, however, for us!
On tient, c'est inimaginable,	One takes up—it's unbelievable—
si peu de place en se serrant!	so little room sitting close together!
Adieu, notre petite table!	Farewell, our little table!
Un même verre était le nôtre;	The same drinking glass was ours;
chacun de nous quand il buvait	each of us, when he drank,
y cherchait les lèvres de l'autre.	searched in it for the lips of the other.
Ah! pauvre ami, comme il m'aimait!	Ah, poor friend—how he loved me!
Adieu, notre petite table!	Farewell, our little table!

I PAGLIACCI
(The Clowns)
1892
music and libretto by Ruggero Leoncavallo (based on a legal case his father heard as a judge)

Stridono lassù
(Ballatella)

from Act I
setting: an Italian village in the province of Calabria, the late 1860s; a street on the outskirts of the village; August; sunset
character: Nedda

Canio and his wife, Nedda, are part of a troupe of travelling players. Canio, the head of the troupe, questions his wife's fidelity, and not without reason. Left alone, Nedda worries about his suspicions, but soon abandons herself to the joy of watching birds whirling in flight above her, envying their unrestricted freedom.

Qual fiamma avea nel guardo!	What fire he had in his gaze!
Gli occhi abbassai	I lowered my eyes
per tema ch'ei leggesse	for fear that he would read
il mio pensier segreto!	my secret thoughts!
Oh! s'ei mi sorprendesse...	Oh, if he were to catch me...
brutale come egli è!	brutal as he is!
Ma basti, or via.	But let that be enough! Away now—
Son questi sogni paurosi e fole!	these are frightening dreams and fairy tales!
O che bel sole di mezz'agosto!	Oh, what beautiful mid-August sunshine!
Io son piena di vita, e,	I am full of life, and,
tutta illanguidita per arcano desìo,	completely languid because of secret desire,
non so che bramo!	I don't know what I desire!
Oh! che volo d'augelli,	Oh, what a flight of birds,
e quante strida!	and how much chirping!
Che chiedon? Dove van?	What are they asking? Where are they going?
Chissà?	Who knows?
La mamma mia,	My mama,
che la buona ventura annunziava,	who used to predict good fortune,
comprendeva il lor canto,	understood their singing,
e a me bambina così cantava:	and she sang to me when I was a child, like this:
Hui!	Ah!
Stridono lassù, liberamente	They—the birds—chirp away
lanciati a vol come frecce,	up there, freely launched in flight
gli augel.	like arrows.
Disfidano le nubi	They defy the clouds
e'l sol cocente,	and the scorching sun,
e vanno per le vie del ciel.	and go through the pathways of heaven.
Lasciateli vagar per l'atmosfera,	Let them roam through the atmosphere,
questi assetati d'azzurro	these who are thirsty for sky
e di splendor:	and for splendor:
seguono anch'essi un sogno,	they also follow a dream,
una chimera,	a fantasy;
e vanno fra le nubi d'or!	and they go among the clouds of gold!
Che incalzi il vento	Should the wind rise
e latri la tempesta,	and the storm howl,
con l'ali aperte	with spread wings
san tutto sfidar;	they know how to defy everything;
la pioggia, i lampi—nulla mai	nothing—the rain, the lightning—
li arresta,	ever stops them,
e vanno sugli abissi e i mar.	and they go over chasms and seas.
Vanno laggiù verso un paese strano	They go far off toward a strange land
che sognan forse	which they imagine, perhaps,
e che cercano in van.	and for which they search in vain.
Ma i boëmi del ciel	But the Bohemians of the sky
seguon l'arcano poter	follow the mysterious force
che li sospinge...	which propels them...
e van!	and they go!

FALSTAFF

1893
music by Giuseppe Verdi
libretto by Arrigo Boito (after plays by William Shakespeare, *The Merry Wives of Windsor* and *Henry IV*)

Sul fil d'un soffio etesio

from Act III, scene 2
setting: Windsor, the reign of Henry IV; the park at Herne's Oak; a moonlit night
character: Nannetta

Thinking he has heard the voice of a fairy, the corpulent old knight, Falstaff, has been wailing that it would be death to anyone who chances to look on such a being. Disguised as Titania, Nannetta appears and calls her fairy band, impersonated by a group of children who answer as a chorus. And all the while Falstaff trembles in mortal fear.

Sul fil d'un soffio etesio	On the breath of an etesian breeze
scorrete, agili larve;	scurry, agile shadows;
fra i rami un baglior cesio	among the branches a bluish-grey glow
d'alba lunare apparve.	of the rising moon has appeared.
Danzate! E il passo blando	Dance! And may the gentle steps
misuri un blando suon,	measure a gentle sound,
le magiche accoppiando carole	combining the magical dances
alla canzon.	with the song.
Erriam sotto la luna	Let us wander beneath the moon,
scegliendo fior da fiore;	choosing flower by flower;
ogni corolla in core	each crown of petals, in its heart,
porta la sua fortuna.	brings its good fortune.
Coi gigli e le vïole	With the lilies and the violets
scriviam de' nomi arcani;	let us write secret names;
dalle fatate mani	from our enchanted hands
germoglino parole…	may words blossom…
parole alluminate di puro argento	words illuminated by pure silver
e d'or…	and by gold…
carmi e malìe.	magic incantations and magic charms.
Le Fate hanno per cifre	The Fairies have, for letters of the alphabet,
i fior.	flowers.

LA BOHÈME

(The Bohemian Life)
1896
music by Giacomo Puccini
libretto by Luigi Illica and Giuseppe Giacoso (after the novel *Scènes de la Vie de Bohème* by Henri Murger)

Mi chiamano Mimì

from Act I
setting: Paris, the Latin Quarter, c. 1830; a garret apartment; Christmas Eve
character: Mimì

Mimì, a seamstress, knocks on the door of a neighboring apartment because her candle has blown out. Rodolfo, a young poet, answers the knock and his own candle flame goes out. He pretends not to find the key that Mimì drops in the darkness, and introduces himself in a poetic discourse. Then he sits in the dark and listens to Mimì's simple words about herself.

Sì. Mi chiamano Mimì,	Yes... They call me Mimi,
ma il mio nome è Lucia.	but my name is Lucia.
La storia mia è breve:	My story is brief:
A tela o a seta	On linen or on silk
ricamo in casa e fuori.	I do embroidery at home and outside.
Son tranquilla e lieta,	I am quiet and cheerful,
ed è mio svago far gigli e rose.	and my hobby is making lilies and roses.
Mi piaccion quelle cose	Those things give me pleasure
che han sì dolce malìa,	which have so much sweet charm,
che parlano d'amor, di primavere,	which speak of love, of springtimes,
che parlano di sogni e di chimere—	which speak of dreams and of fantasies—
quelle cose che han nome poesia.	those things which are called poetry.
Lei m'intende?	Do you understand me?
Mi chiamano Mimì.	They call me Mimi.
Il perchè non so.	Why, I don't know.
Sola, mi fo il pranzo da me stessa.	Alone, I make meals at home by myself.
Non vado sempre a messa	I do not always go to mass
ma prego assai il Signor.	but I pray a great deal to the Lord.
Vivo sola, soletta,	I live alone—all alone—
là in una bianca cameretta;	there, in a clean little room;
guardo sui tetti e in cielo.	I look out on the rooftops and the sky.
Ma quando vien lo sgelo	But when the spring thaw comes
il primo sole è mio...	the early sun is mine...
il primo bacio dell'aprile è mio!	the first kiss of April is mine!
Germoglia in un vaso una rosa...	A rose blooms in a vase...
foglia a foglia la spio!	petal by petal I watch over it!
Così gentil il profumo d'un fior!	How delicate, the scent of a flower!
Ma i fior ch'io faccio, ahimè!	But the flowers that I make, alas,
non hanno odore!	do not have fragrance!
Altro di me non le saprei narrare.	I would not know how to tell you anything else about me.
Sono la sua vicina	I am your neighbor
che la vien fuori d'ora a importunare.	who comes unexpectedly to interrupt you.

Quando men vo

from Act II
setting: Paris, c. 1830; the Latin Quarter; Café Momus; Christmas Eve
character: Musetta

Musetta is a coquette and a café singer. Though she enters the Café Momus on Christmas Eve with an aging admirer in tow, she bursts into song to force the attention of her old lover, Marcello.

Quando men vo soletta per la via	When I go out alone in the street
la gente sosta e mira...	people stop and stare...
e la bellezza mia tutta ricerca in me	and they all study in me my beauty
da capo a piè.	from head to foot.
Ed assaporo allor la bramosia sottil	And then I savor the subtle longing
che da gl'occhi traspira;	that comes from their eyes;
e dai palesi vezzi intender sa	they know how to appreciate, beneath
alle occulte beltà.	obvious charms, all the hidden beauty.
Così l'effluvio del desìo	Thus the flow of desire
tutta m'aggira;	completely surrounds me;
felice mi fa!	it makes me happy!
E tu che sai, che memori	And you who know, who remember
e ti struggi,	and are melting with passion—
da me tanto rifuggi?	you avoid me so?
So ben: le angoscie tue	I know well: your sufferings—
non le vuoi dir;	you don't want to tell them;
so ben,	I know well,
ma ti senti morir!	but you feel like you're dying!

Donde lieta uscì

from Act III
setting: Paris, c. 1830; outside a tavern near the city gate; February; before dawn; snow
character: Mimì

Rodolfo has left Mimì. She is ill. On a cold winter morning she makes her way to an inn where their mutual friend, Marcello, is staying. She seeks Marcello's company and advice, and is surprised to find Rodolfo also at the tavern. When the lovers meet Mimì sings this touching farewell.

Donde lieta uscì	*From the place she left, happy*
al tuo grido d'amore,	*at your declaration of love,*
torna sola Mimì	*Mimì returns alone*
al solitario nido.	*to her solitary nest.*
Ritorna un'altra volta	*She goes back once again*
a intesser finti fior!	*to make unreal flowers!*
Addio, senza rancor.	*Farewell, without remorse.*
Ascolta.	*Wait...*
Le poche robe aduna	*Gather together the few things*
che lasciai sparse.	*that I left scattered around.*
Nel mio cassetto stan chiusi	*Shut in my drawer are*
quel cerchietto d'or,	*that gold ring*
e il libro di preghiere.	*and the prayer book.*
Involgi tutto quanto in un grembiale	*Wrap them all up in a smock*
e manderò il portiere...	*and I will send the porter...*
Bada... sotto il guanciale	*Careful... under the pillow*
c'è la cuffietta rosa.	*there is the pink bonnet.*
Se vuoi,	*If you wish,*
serbarla a ricordo d'amor!	*keep it in remembrance of love!*
Addio, senza rancor.	*Farewell, without remorse.*

MADAMA BUTTERFLY

1904
music by Giacomo Puccini
libretto by Luigi Illica and Giuseppe Giacoso (after the play by David Belasco, which was based on a story by John Luther Long)

Un bel dì vedremo

from Act II
setting: Nagasaki, Japan, c. 1900; Butterfly's house
character: Cio-Cio-San (Madama Butterfly)

Cio-Cio-San has been abandoned by her American husband, Lieutenant B. F. Pinkerton. Three years have passed, and her faithful servant, Suzuki, pleads with her to forget him and move on to a new life. Butterfly berates her and sings of how it will be when her husband returns.

Piangi? Perchè?	*You're crying? Why?*
Ah, la fede ti manca!	*Ah, faith is lacking in you!*
Senti.	*Listen.*
Un bel dì vedremo	*One beautiful day we will see*
levarsi un fil di fumo	*a thread of smoke rise*
sull'estremo confin del mare.	*on the far horizon of the sea.*
E poi la nave appare.	*And then the ship appears.*
Poi la nave bianca entra nel porto,	*Then the white ship enters the port,*
romba il suo saluto.	*roars its salute.*
Vedi? È venuto!	*You see? He has come!*

Io non gli scendo incontro—io no.	I will not go down to meet him—not I.
Mi metto là	I will position myself there
sul ciglio del colle	on the edge of the hill
e aspetto gran tempo;	and wait a long time;
e non mi pesa,	and the long wait
la lunga attesa.	will not be hard on me.
E… uscito dalla folla cittadina	And… having emerged from the town crowd,
un uomo, un picciol punto	a man—a tiny speck—
s'avvia per la collina.	sets out for the hill.
Chi sarà?	Who will it be?
E come sarà giunto	And when he has arrived,
che dirà?	what will he say?
Chiamerà Butterfly dalla lontana.	He will call Butterfly from the distance.
Io senza dar risposta	I, without giving answer,
me ne starò nascosta	will remain concealed from him—
un po' per celia	a bit in play
e un po' per non morire	and a bit so as not to die
al primo incontro.	at the first reunion.
Ed egli alquanto in pena chiamerà:	And he, somewhat anxious, will call:
Piccina mogliettina,	"dear little wife,"
olezzo di verbena,	"fragrance of verbena"—
i nomi che mi dava al suo venire.	the names he used to call me whenever he arrived.
Tutto questo avverrà, te lo prometto.	All this will happen, I promise you.
Tienti la tua paura;	Persist in your fear;
io con sicura fede l'aspetto.	I, with sure faith, await him!

GIANNI SCHICCHI

1918
part three of *Il Trittico (The Trilogy)*
music by Giacomo Puccini
libretto by Giovacchino Forzano (based on an episode in Dante's *Inferno*)

O mio babbino caro

in one act
setting: Florence, 1299; the house of the recently deceased Buoso Donati
character: Lauretta

The relatives of Buoso Donati have been left out of the old man's will. Rinuccio, his nephew, has a girl friend, Lauretta, whose father, Gianni Schicchi, is a very clever rogue. Rinuccio begs Schicchi to help the family, but he refuses because of their condescension toward him and his daughter. Lauretta pleads convincingly with her father on Rinuccio's behalf.

O mio babbino caro,	*Oh my dear daddy,*
mi piace, è bello;	*he pleases me; he is handsome!*
vo' andare in Porta Rossa	*I want to go to Porta Rossa**
a comperar l'anello!	*to buy the ring!*
Sì, ci voglio andare!	*Yes, I want to go there!*
E se l'amassi indarno,	*And if I should love him in vain,*
andrei sul Ponte Vecchio,	*I would go to the Ponte Vecchio,***
ma per buttarmi in Arno!	*but in order to throw myself into the Arno!****
Mi struggo e mi tormento!	*I am feeling tortured and tormented!*
O Dio, vorrei morir!	*Oh God, I should like to die!*
Babbo, pietà!	*Daddy, have pity!*

   * Porta Rossa ("Red Gate") refers to a marketplace off Via Porta Rossa in central Florence.
  **Il Ponte Vecchio (the "Old Bridge") in Florence was the only bridge over the Arno until 1218, and the only one to survive destruction there during World War II.
***The Arno, one of the largest rivers of Italy, bisects Florence where the river is narrowest.

TURANDOT

1926
music by Giacomo Puccini
libretto by Giuseppe Adami and Renato Simoni (after an adaptation by Schiller of Count Carlo Gozzi's play *Turandotte*, also perhaps after *The Arabian Nights*)

The opera was incomplete at the time of Puccini's death in 1924; the last scene was completed by Franco Alfano, later abridged by Arturo Toscanini.

Signore, ascolta!

from Act I
setting: ancient, legendary Peking; a square outside the walls of the Imperial Palace
character: Liù

Calaf, son of Timur, the exiled king of the Tartars, is reunited with his father and Timur's faithful servant, Liù. Calaf, like many before him, falls in love with the beautiful Princess Turandot who will only wed the man who can answer three riddles. Death awaits all who fail in their quest. In this aria Liù, who has long been secretly in love with Calaf, begs him, for his father's sake and her own, not to sacrifice his life.

Signore, ascolta!	*My lord, listen!*
Ah, signore, ascolta!	*Ah, my lord, listen!*
Liù non regge più!	*Liù will bear no more!*
Si spezza il cuor!	*Her heart is breaking!*
Ahimè, quanto cammino	*Alas, what a long road I have travelled*
col tuo nome nell'anima,	*with your name in my soul,*
col nome tuo sulle labbra!	*with your name on my lips!*
Ma se il tuo destino,	*But if your fate*
doman, sarà deciso,	*will be decided tomorrow,*
noi morrem sulla strada dell'esilio!	*we will die on the path of exile!*
Ei perderà suo figlio…	*He will lose his son…*
io l'ombra d'un sorriso!	*I, the trace of a smile!*
Liù non regge più!	*Liù will bear no more!*
Ah, pietà!	*Ah, have pity!*

Tu che di gel sei cinta

from Act III, scene 1
setting: ancient, legendary Peking; the vast garden of the Imperial Palace; night
character: Liù

Calaf has answered Princess Turandot's riddles and has won the right to marry her, which infuriates and terrifies her. In concession, he has told her that if she can learn his name before dawn he will still forfeit his life. Timur and Liù are tortured, but neither reveals the name. In defiance, Liù tells the Princess that she loves Calaf and her silence will be the final gift of that love. At the end of the aria, she seizes the dagger of a soldier and stabs herself.

Tu che di gel sei cinta,	*You, who with ice are girded,*
da tanta fiamma vinta,	*conquered by so much burning passion,*
l'amerai anche tu!	*you will love him—you too!*
Prima di questa aurora,	*Before this dawn*
io chiudo stanca gli occhi,	*I, weary, will close my eyes*
perchè egli vinca ancora…	*so that he may be victorious again…*
ei vinca ancora…	*he may be victorious again…*
per non vederlo più!	*so as never to see him again!*

THE MEDIUM
1946
music and libretto by Gian Carlo Menotti

The Black Swan

from Act I
setting: the outskirts of a large city, the present (1940s); the parlor of Madame Flora's flat
character: Monica

Baba, also known as Madame Flora, is a down-on-her-luck alcoholic who pretends to be a spiritualist. In the midst of a séance she throws her customers out when she herself feels an unexplained presence in the room. She sinks into a fitful stupor as her daughter, Monica, cradles her in her arms, trying to comfort her with this haunting lullaby.

Monica's Waltz

from Act II
setting: the outskirts of a large city, the present (1940s); the parlor of Madame Flora's flat
character: Monica

Monica, Baba's daughter, and Toby, a mute gypsy boy pulled in off the streets, have enjoyed an endless series of fantasy games together. But now childhood affection, at least for Toby, is blossoming into love.

THE BALLAD OF BABY DOE
1956
music by Douglas Moore
libretto by John Latouche (based on the life of Baby Doe Tabor, 1854-1935)

Willow Song

from Act I, scene 2
setting: Leadville, Colorado, 1880; outside the Clarendon Hotel; late evening
character: Baby Doe

Baby Doe is new in Leadville, having just shaken the dust of Central City and an unfortunate marriage. She sits in the hotel lobby late in the evening playing the piano and singing, not knowing that Horace Tabor, the silver tycoon, is listening.

The Silver Aria

from Act I, scene 6
setting: Washington, D.C., 1883; a suite in the Willard Hotel
character: Baby Doe

At the wedding reception for Senator Horace Tabor and his new wife, Baby Doe, the senator is questioned about forthcoming legislation that might disturb the financial status of silver. The lovely bride naively but eloquently interrupts the conversation, rhapsodizing for all to hear on the wonders of silver.

TARTUFFE
1980
music and libretto by Kirke Mechem (after the play by Moliére)

Fair Robin I love

from Act I
setting: Paris, the 17th century; the house of Orgon, a wealthy aristocrat
character: Dorine

Dorine, the saucy maid to Orgon's daughter, Mariane, sings a song to her mistress, attempting to educate her on the lighter side of romance. The words of the aria are from John Dryden's "Amphitryon" (1690); the name "Robin" was "Iris" in the original poem.

V'adoro, pupille

from
GIULIO CESARE

George Frideric Handel

Porgi, amor

from
LE NOZZE DI FIGARO

Wolfgang Amadeus Mozart

* Appoggiatura optional

Dove sono i bei momenti

from
LE NOZZE DI FIGARO

Wolfgang Amadeus Mozart

Andante
CONTESSA:

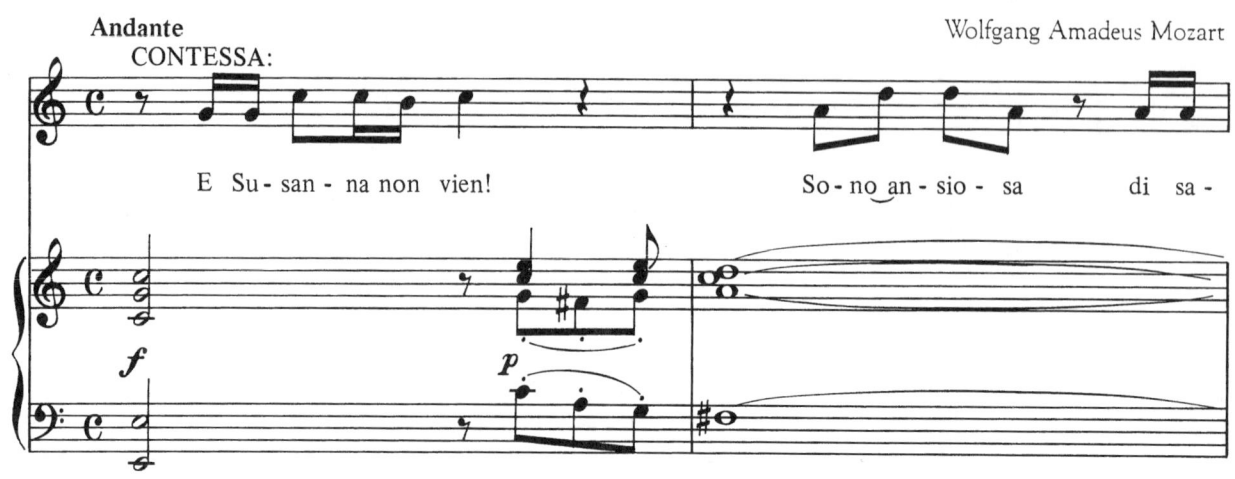

E Su-san-na non vien! So-no an-sio-sa di sa-

per co-me il Con-te ac-col-se la pro-po-sta.

Al-quan-to ar-di-to il pro-get-to mi par, e ad u-no spo-so sì vi-

*Appoggiatura recommended

Deh vieni, non tardar

from
LE NOZZE DI FIGARO

Wolfgang Amadeus Mozart

*Appoggiatura recommended

Bester Jüngling

from
DER SCHAUSPIELDIREKTOR

Wolfgang Amadeus Mozart

FRÄULEIN SILBERKLANG:

Bes - ter Jüng-ling, mit Ent - zük-ken nehm' ich dei - ne Lie - be— an, da in

Batti, batti, o bel Masetto

from
DON GIOVANNI

Wolfgang Amadeus Mozart

*Appoggiatura recommended

attacca l'aria

Vedrai, carino

from
DON GIOVANNI

Wolfgang Amadeus Mozart

O wär' ich schon mit dir vereint

from
FIDELIO

Ludwig van Beethoven

70

Kommt ein schlanker Bursch gegangen

from
DER FREISCHÜTZ

Carl Maria von Weber

Caro nome

from
RIGOLETTO

Giuseppe Verdi

* This cadenza has long been traditionally sung in place of the original cadenza at this spot.

The Jewel Song

from
FAUST

Charles Gounod

Ah! Je veux vivre

from
ROMÉO ET JULIETTE

Charles Gounod

Elle a fui, la tourterelle!

from
LES CONTES D'HOFFMANN

Jacques Offenbach

Adieu, notre petite table

from
MANON

Jules Massenet

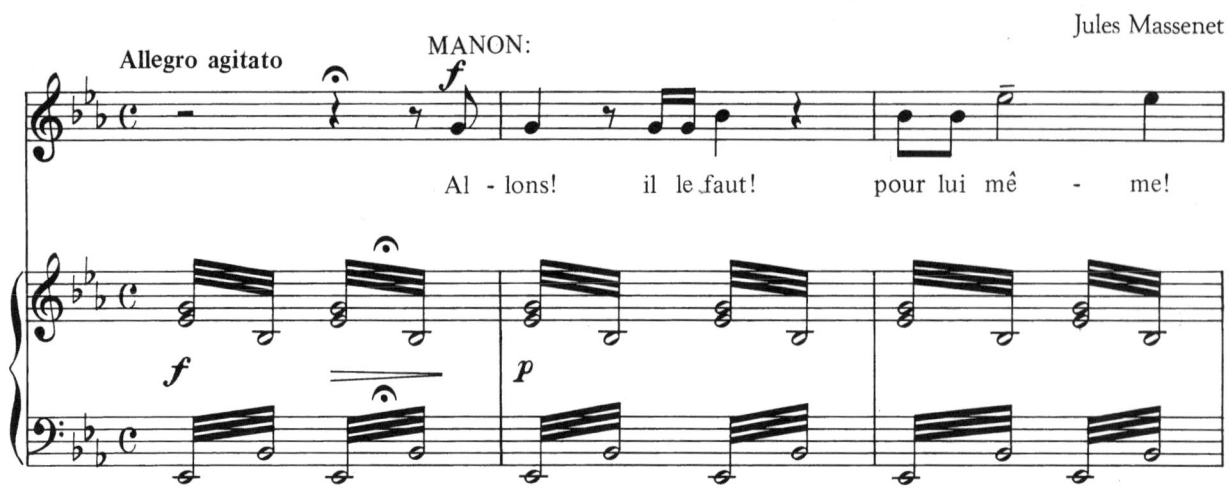

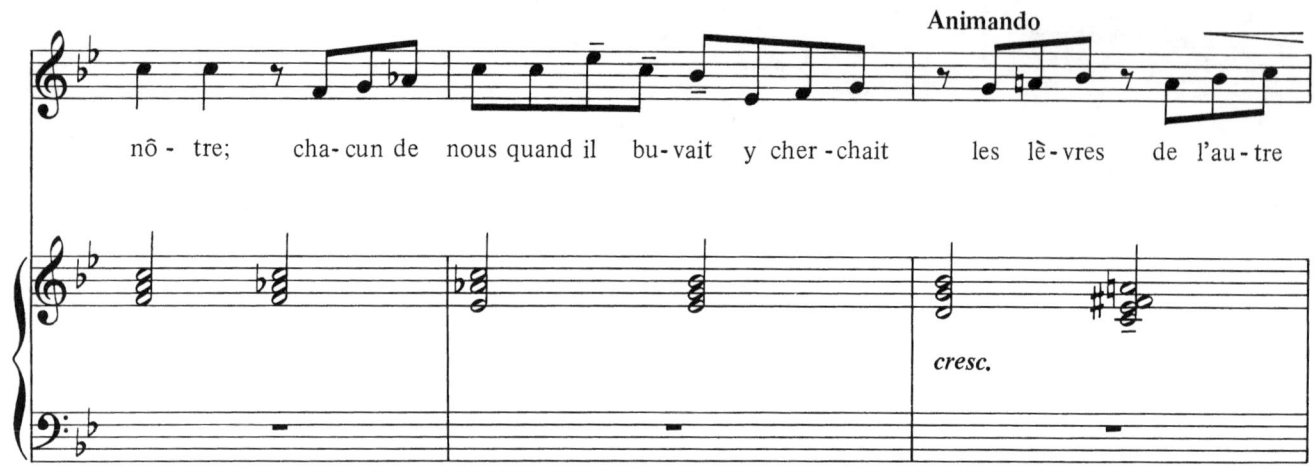
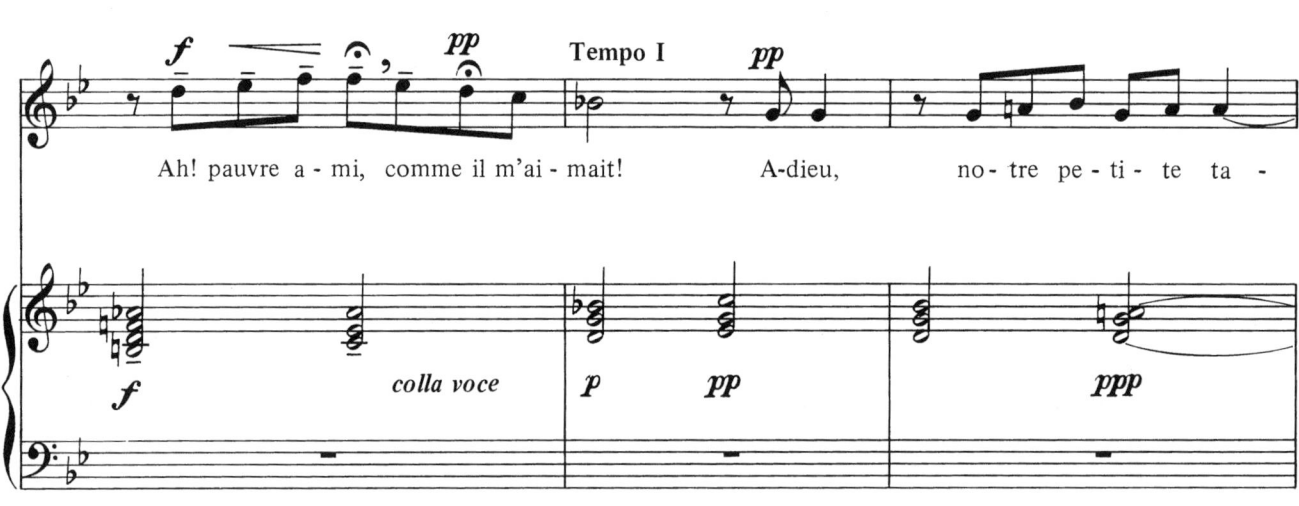

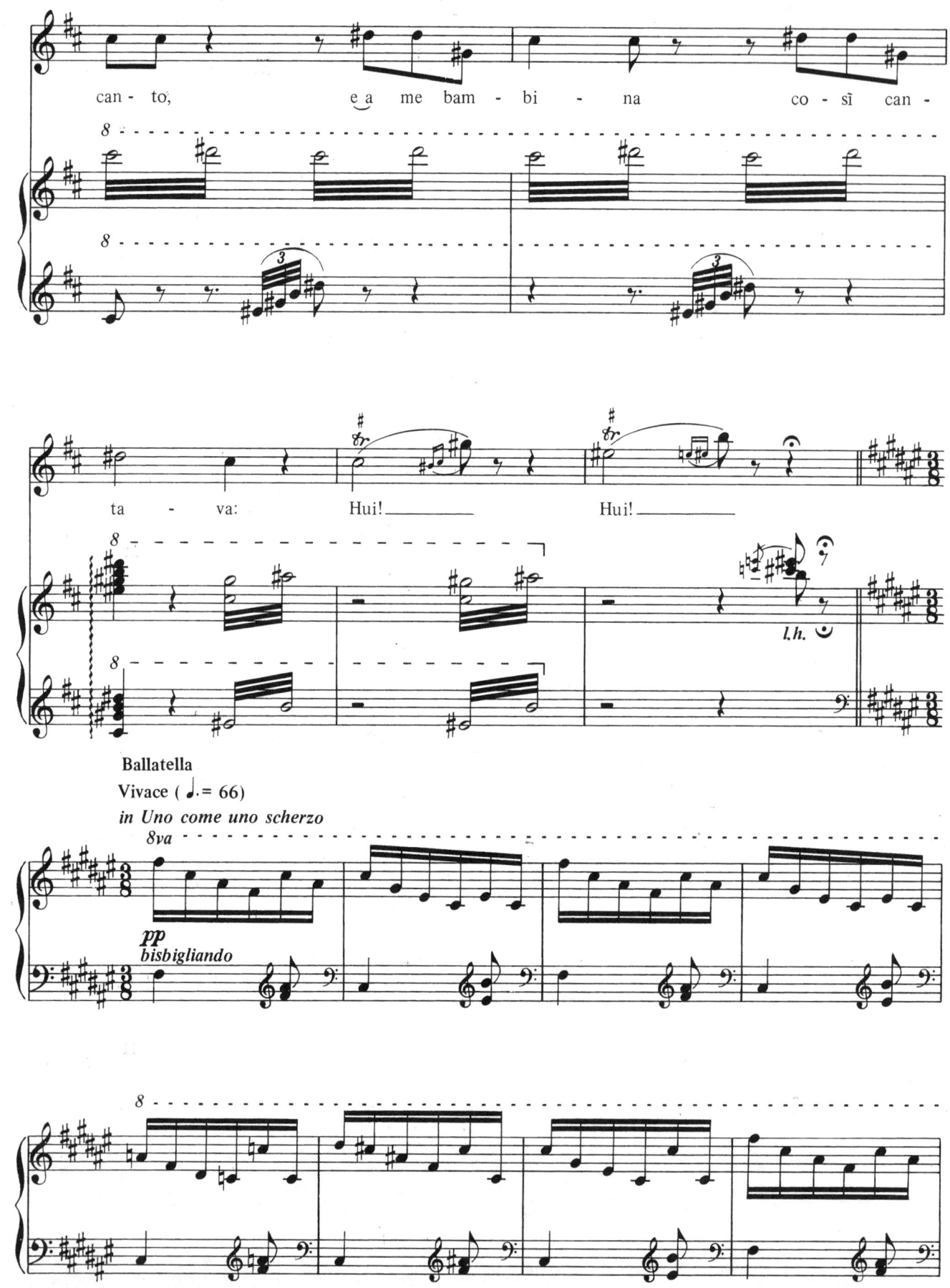

Mi chiamano Mimì

from
LA BOHÈME

Giacomo Puccini

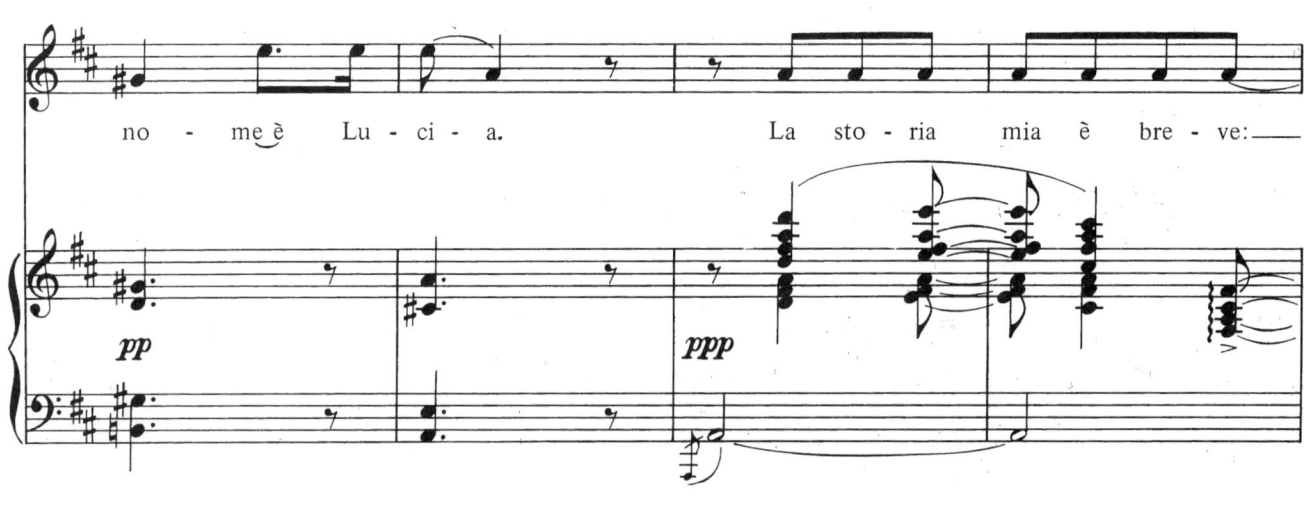

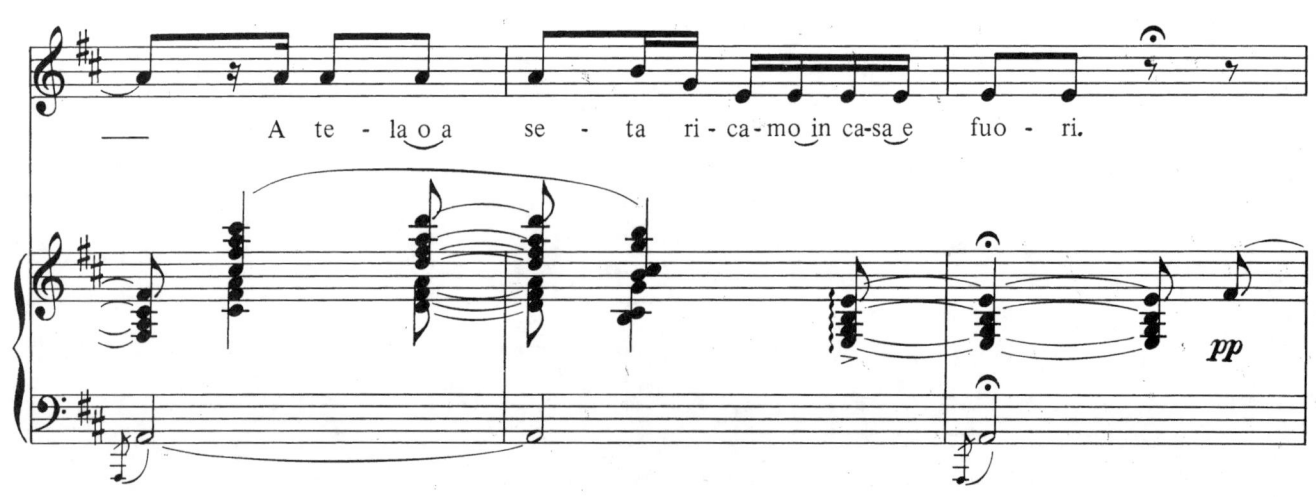

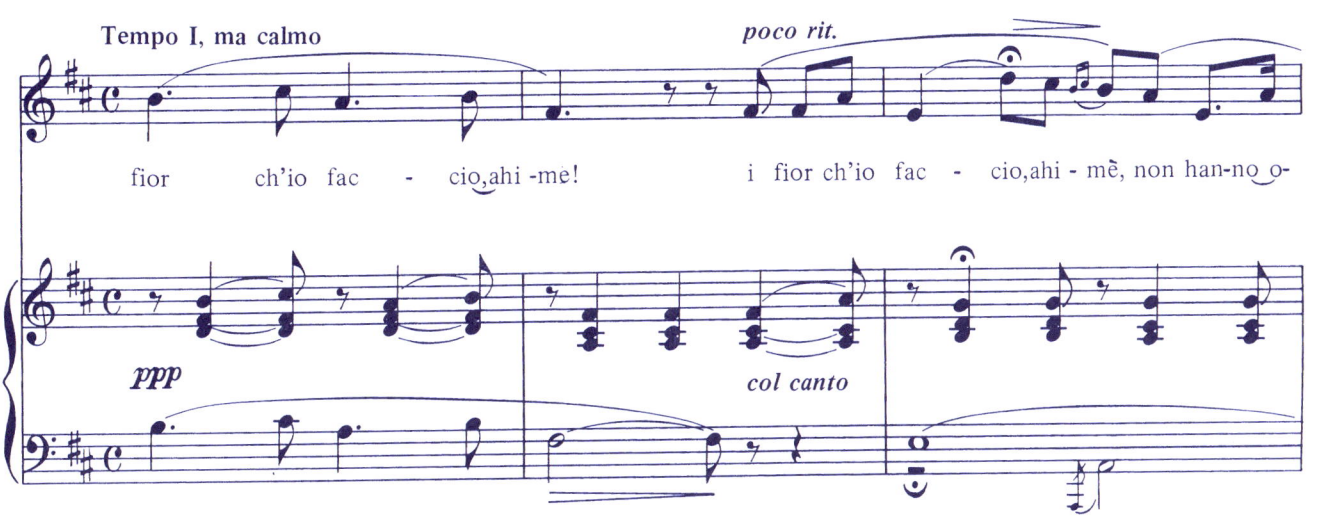

Quando men vo

from
LA BOHÈME

Giacomo Puccini

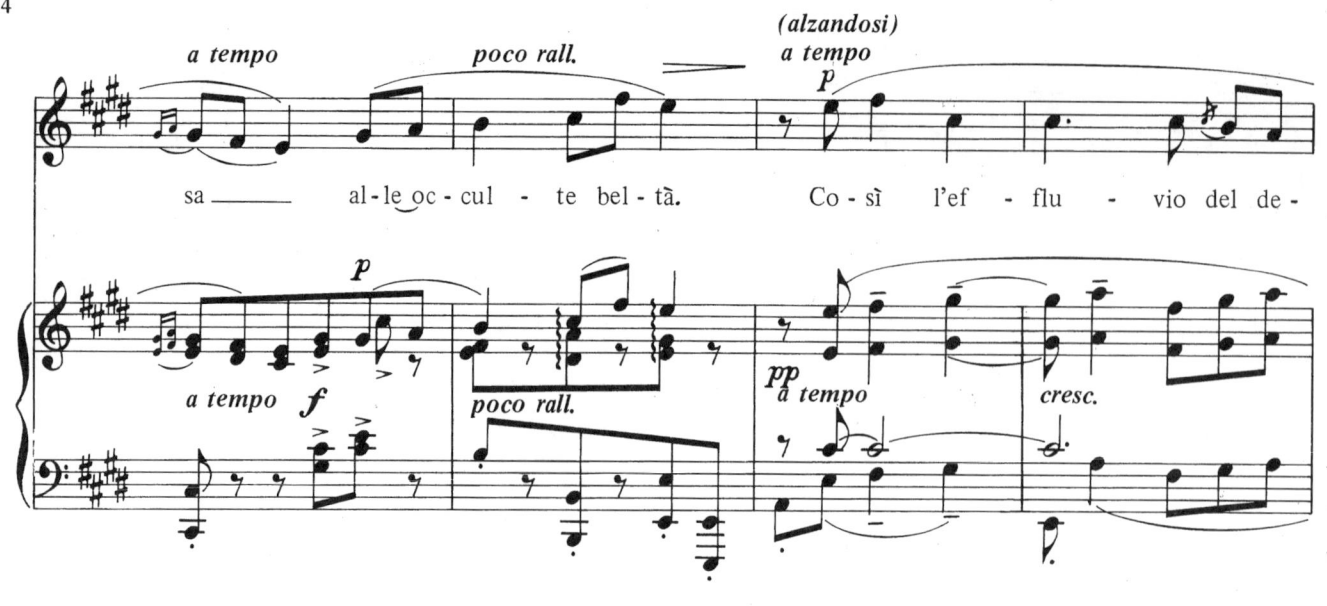
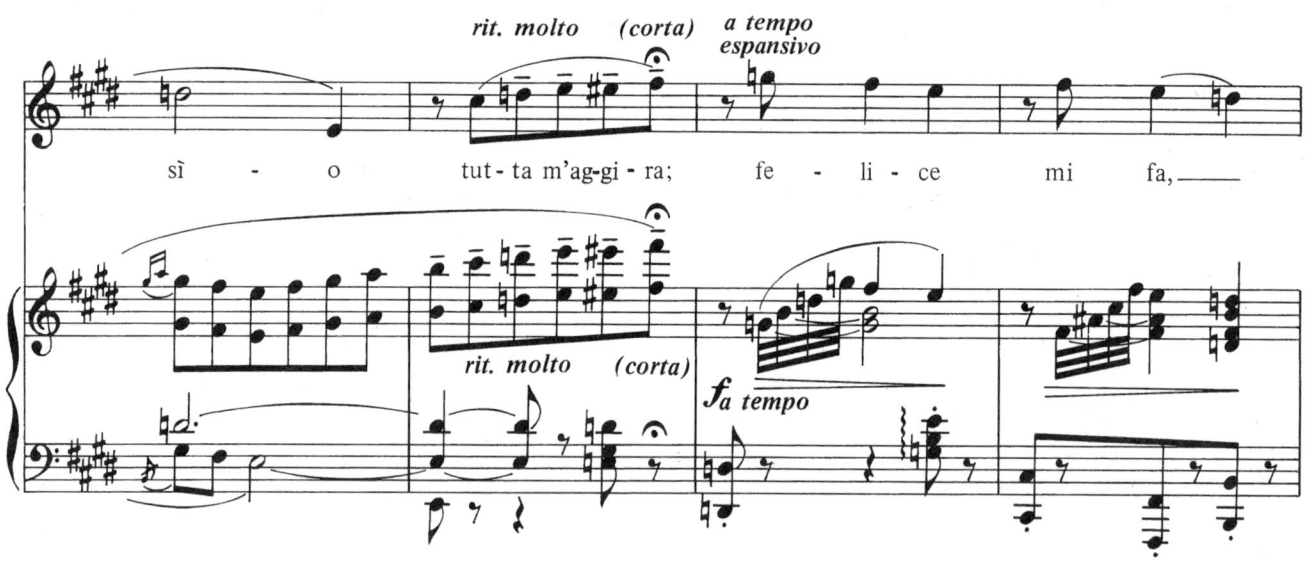

Donde lieta

from
LA BOHÈME

Giacomo Puccini

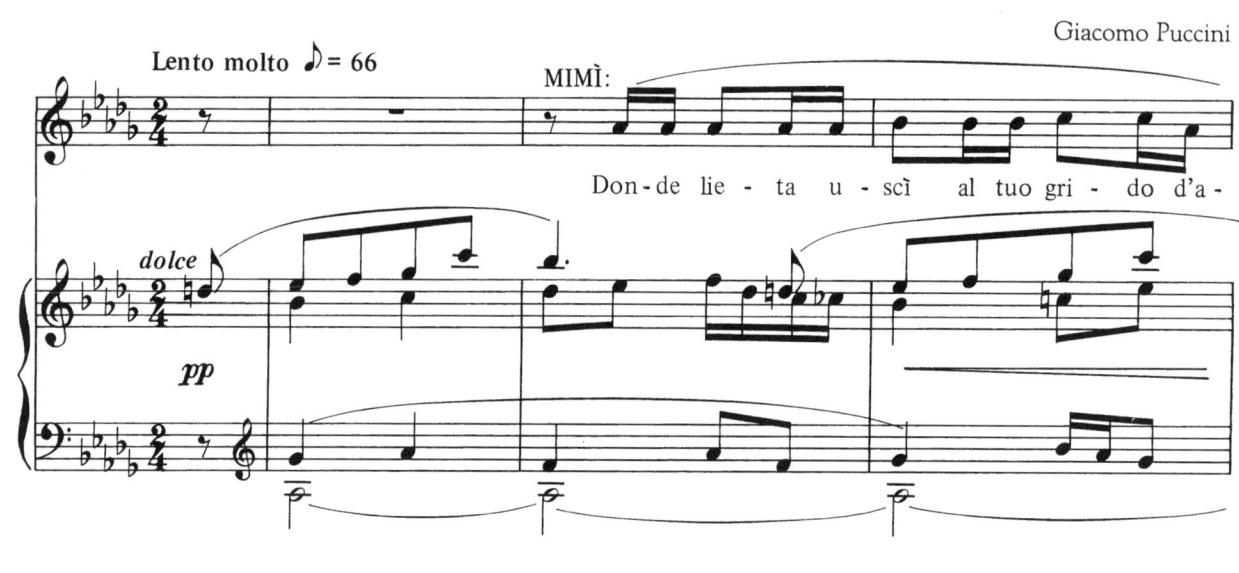
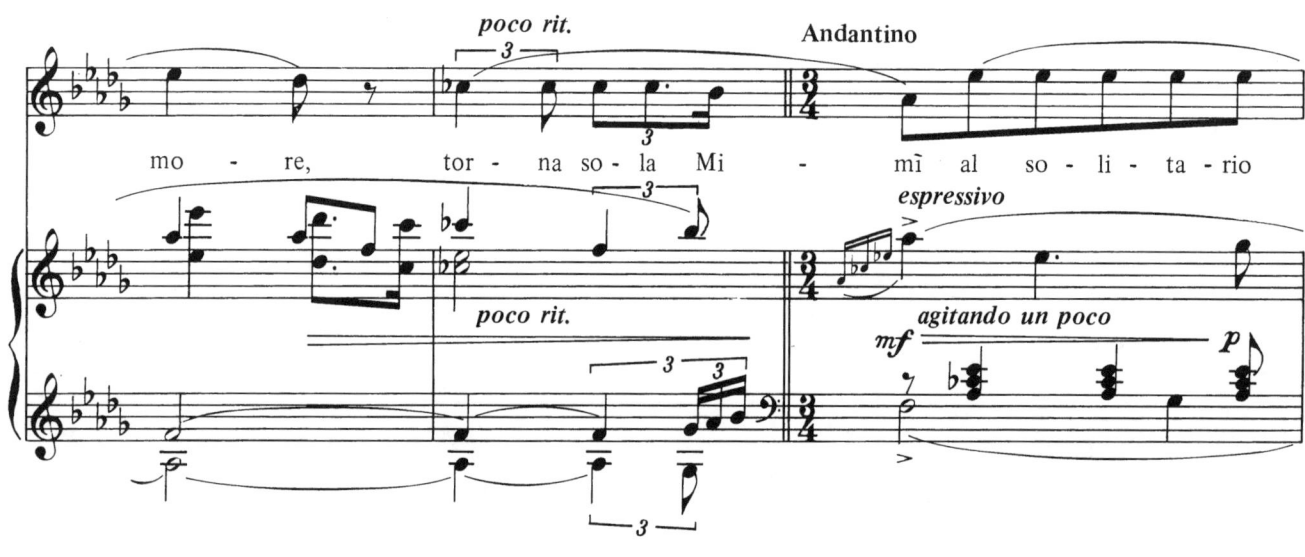

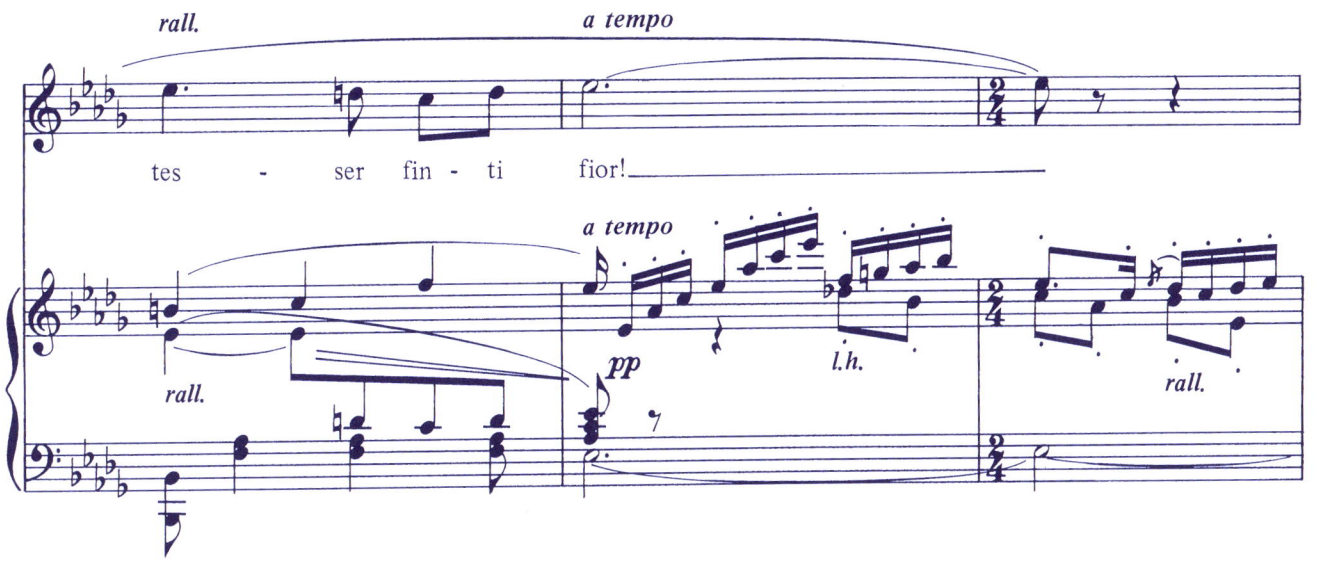

Un bel dì vedremo
from
MADAMA BUTTERFLY

Giacomo Puccini

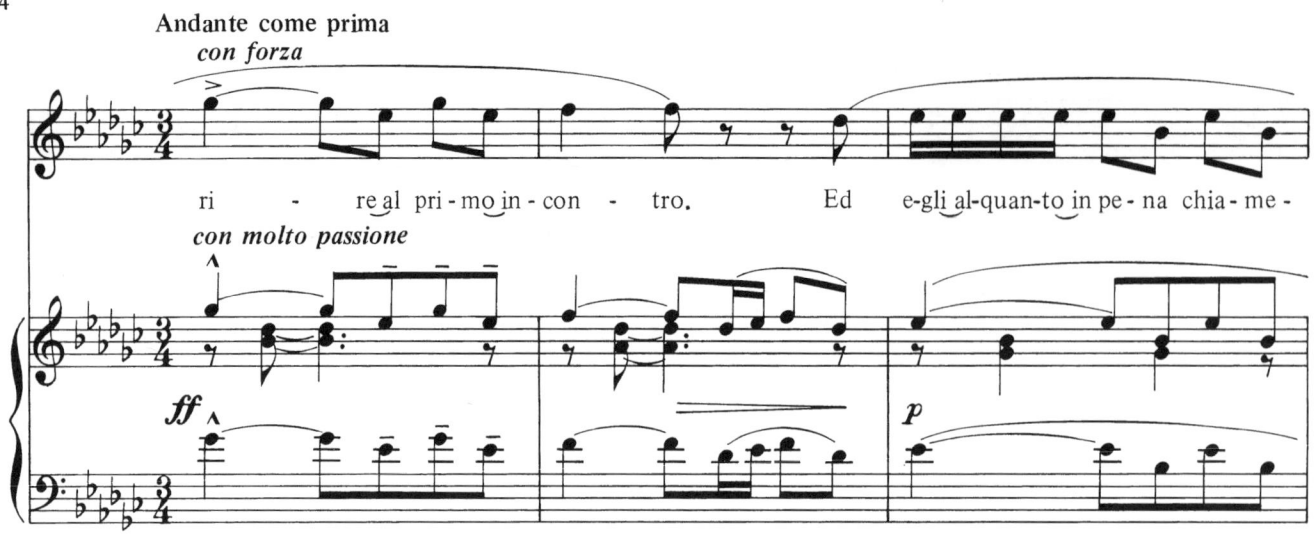
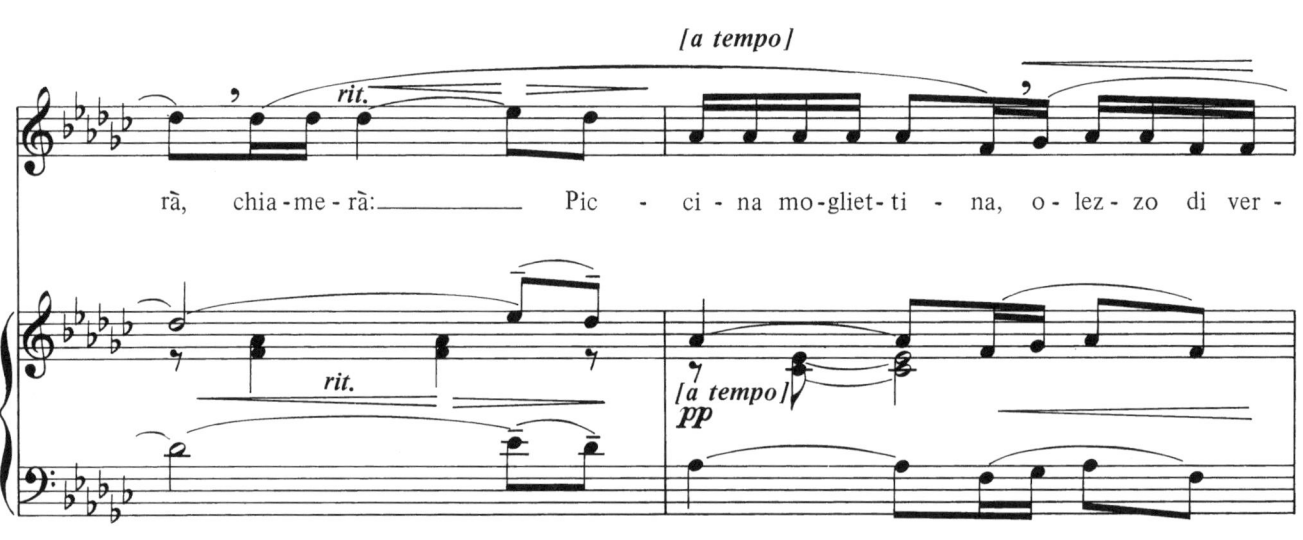

O mio babbino caro

from
GIANNI SCHICCHI

Giacomo Puccini

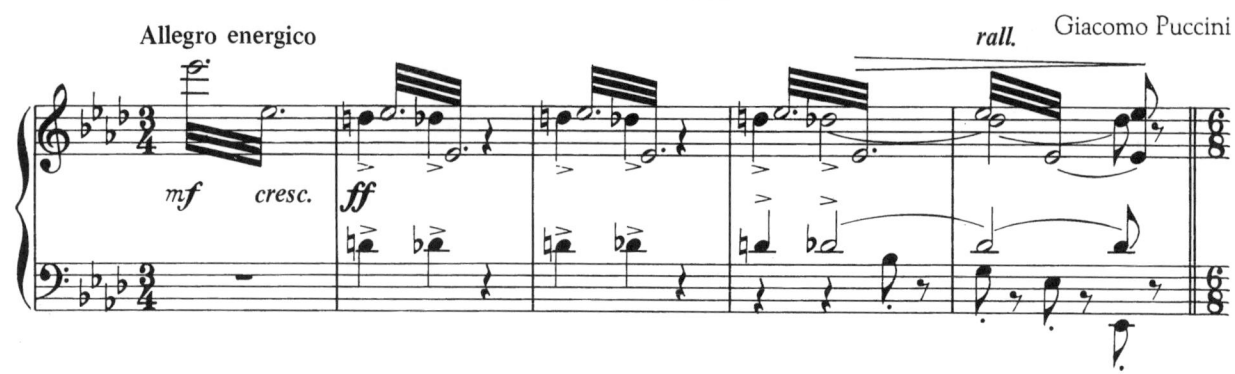

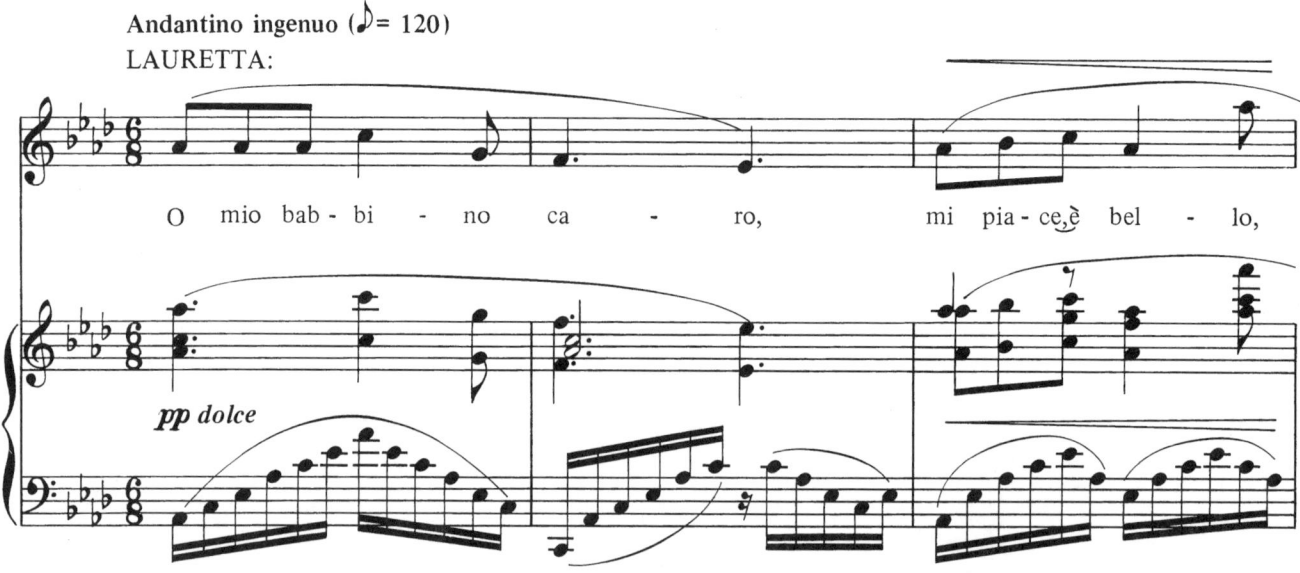

Copyright © 1918 by G. Ricordi & Co.

Signore, ascolta!

from
TURANDOT

Giacomo Puccini

Copyright © 1926 by G. Ricordi & Co.

The Black Swan

from
THE MEDIUM

Gian Carlo Menotti

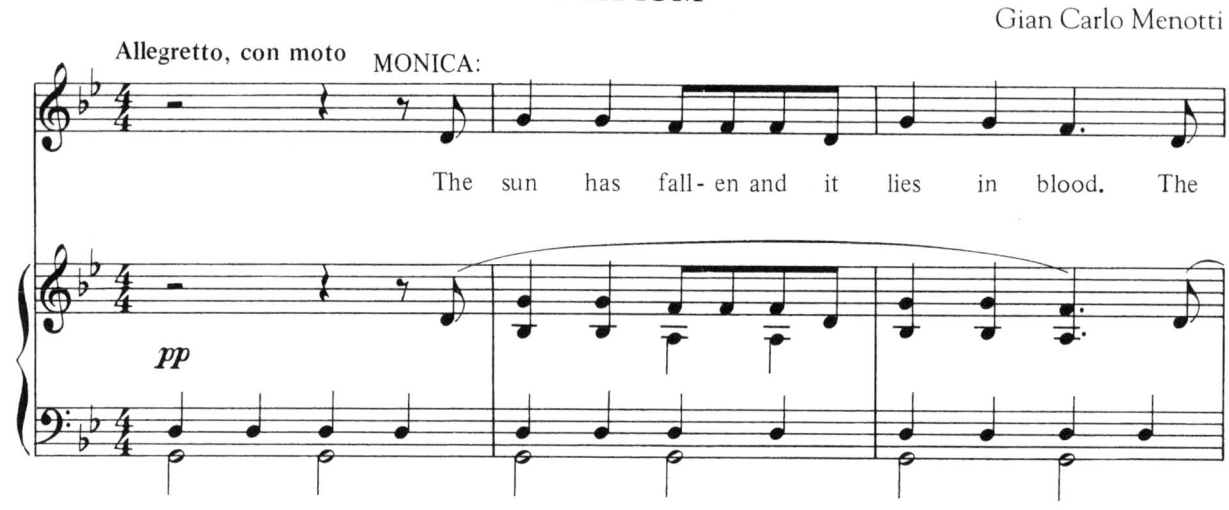

Copyright © 1947 by G. Schirmer, Inc. (ASCAP) New York, NY
International Copyright Secured. All Rights Reserved.
Warning: Unauthorized reproduction of this publication is
prohibited by Federal Law and subject to criminal prosecution.

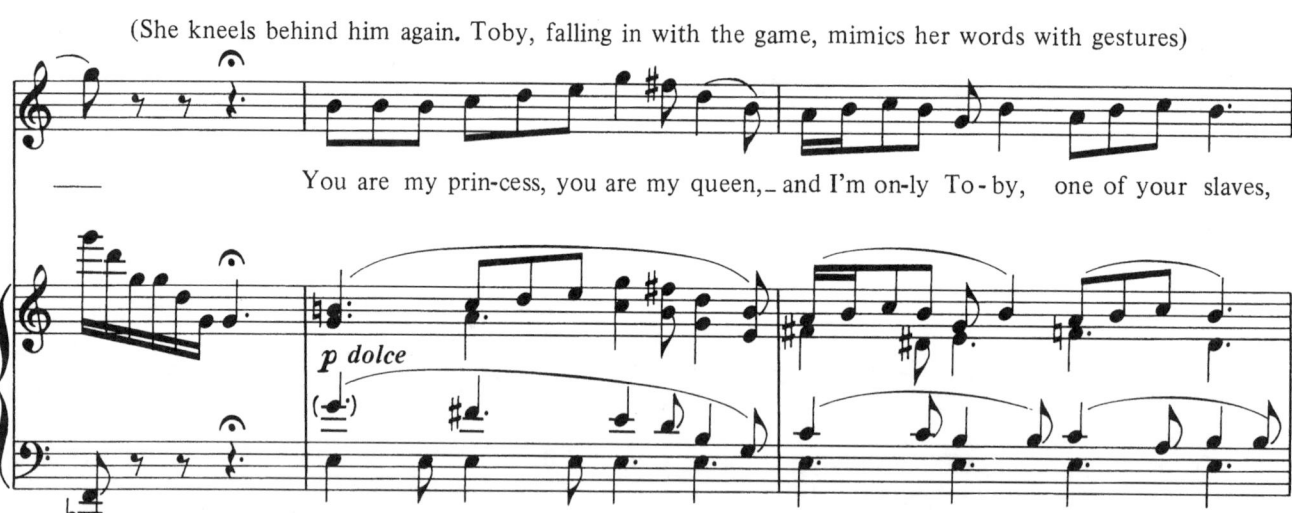

(She kneels behind him again. Toby, falling in with the game, mimics her words with gestures)

Willow Song
from
THE BALLAD OF BABY DOE

Douglas Moore

The Silver Aria

from
THE BALLAD OF BABY DOE

Douglas Moore

Copyright © 1956 by Douglas S. Moore and John Latouche
Copyright Renewed
Chappell & Co., Owners of Publication and Allied Rights throughout the World.
International Copyright Secured   All Rights Reserved
Unauthorized copying, arranging, adapting, recording or public performance is an infringement of copyright.
Infringers are liable under the law.

196

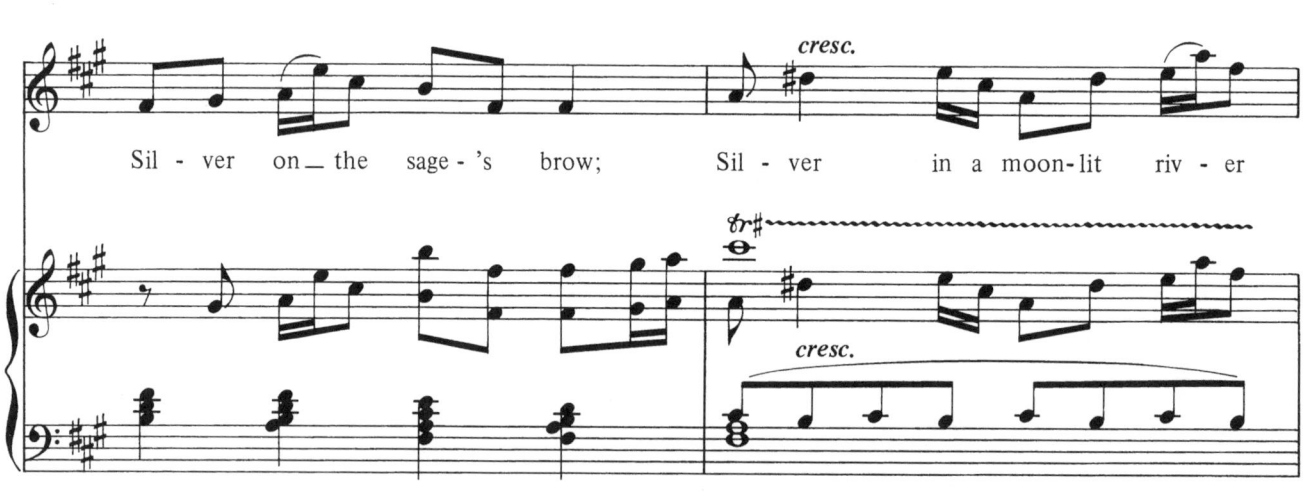

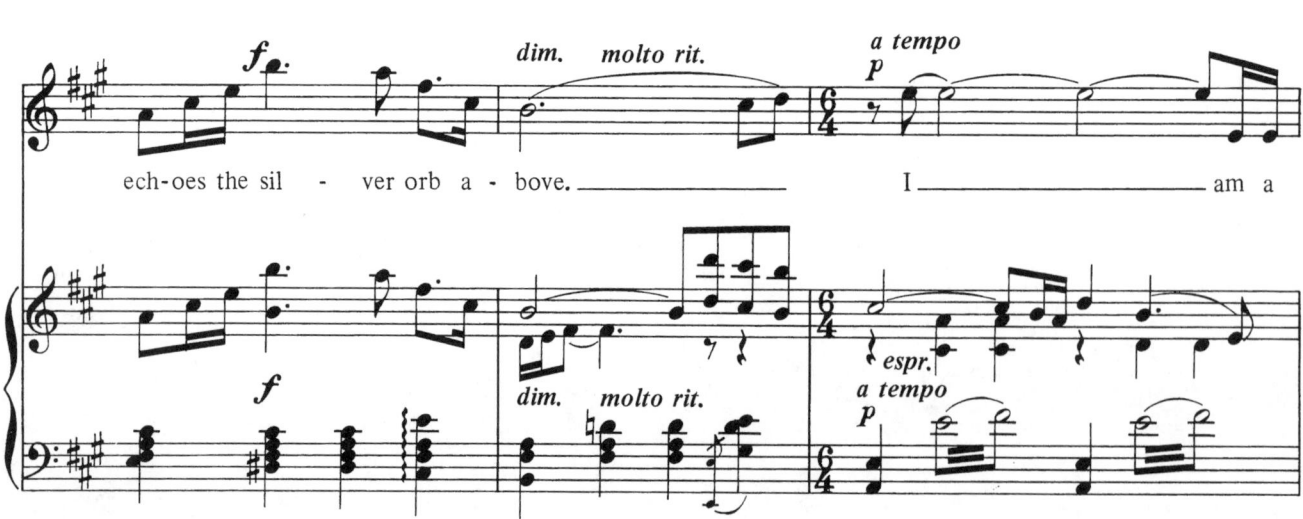

Fair Robin I love

from
TARTUFFE

Kirke Mechem

Copyright © 1980 by G. Schirmer, Inc. (ASCAP) New York, NY
International Copyright Secured.   All Rights Reserved.

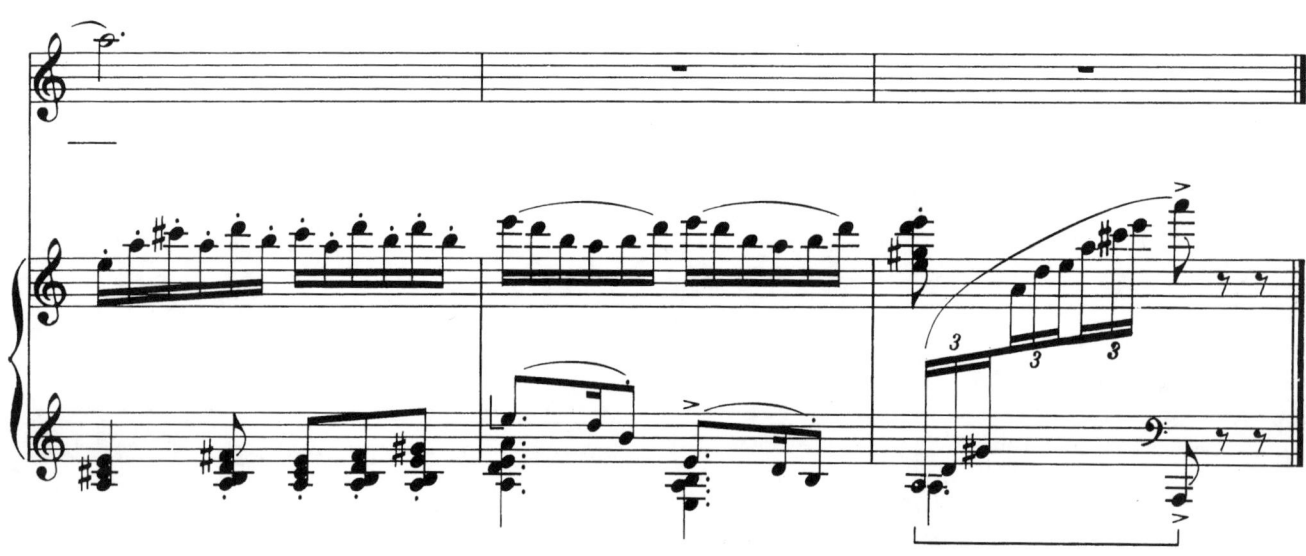

G. SCHIRMER OPERA ANTHOLOGY

DICTION COACH
ARIAS FOR
SOPRANO

International Phonetic Alphabet and Diction Lessons
Recorded by a Professional, Native Speaker Coach

Diction Recordings

Corradina Caporello, Italian
Kathryn LaBouff, English
Irene Spiegelman, German
Pierre Vallet, French

International Phonetic Alphabet

Martha Gerhart, Italian and French
Kathryn LaBouff, English
Irene Spiegelman, German

Copyright © 2008 by G. Schirmer, Inc. (ASCAP) New York, NY
International Copyright Secured. All Rights Reserved.
Warning: Unauthorized reproduction of this publication is
prohibited by Federal law and subject to criminal prosecution.

PREFACE

What a wonderful opportunity for singers these volumes represent. The diction coaches recorded on the companion CDs are from the staffs of the Metropolitan Opera and The Juilliard School, whose specialty is working with singers. I personally have had the opportunity to study Italian with Ms. Caporello and have experienced the sheer delight of learning operatic texts with a linguist who is devoted to the art of singing.

There are two versions of the text recorded for each aria.

1. Recitation

The coach speaks the text of the aria as an actor would speak it, using spoken diction and capturing the mood. The guttural "R" is pronounced as in speech in French and German. Even in these free recitations, these experienced coaches are obviously informed as to how the text relates to the musical setting.

2. Diction Lessons

Dividing the text of the aria into short phrases, the coach speaks a line at a time very slowly and deliberately, without interpretation, making each word sound distinct. Time is allowed for the repetition of each phrase. In this slow version the French and German coaches adapt the guttural "R" in a manner appropriate for opera singers. The coaches in all languages make small adjustments recommended for singers in these slowly enunciated diction lessons, including elisions and liaisons between word sounds as related to the sung phrase.

There is not one universally used approach to International Phonetic Alphabet. The article before each language should be studied carefully for comprehension of the specific approach to IPA for each language in this edition.

The diction recordings can be used in many ways but a highly recommended plan is this. After carefully working regularly with the recorded diction lesson and the related IPA over several days, one should be able to reach fluency in the aria text. As an exercise separate from singing the aria, the singer should then speak the text freely, as in the diction coach's recitation. The singer likely will be inspired by the recitations recorded by the diction coaches, but after pronunciation is mastered might even begin to discover informed and individual interpretations in reciting the aria text.

By paying attention to the libretto of an aria, or an entire role, apart from the music, the opera singer can begin to understand character and interpretation in a way that would not be possible if the text is only considered by singing it. Just as an actor explores a script and a character from various historical, intellectual and emotional angles, so must the opera singer. Understanding the stated and unstated meanings of the text is fundamental in becoming a convincing actor on the opera stage, or on the opera audition stage. But the opera singer is only half done. After a thorough exploration of the words, one must discover how the composer interpreted the text and how best to express that interpretation. In great music for the opera stage, that exploration can be a fascinating lifetime journey.

Robert L. Larsen
June, 2008

ARIA TEXTS
CONTENTS

208	CD Track List		**GIULIO CESARE**
210	About Italian IPA	221	V'adoro, pupille
235	About French IPA		
247	About German IPA		**MADAMA BUTTERFLY**
255	About English IPA	221	Un bel dì vedremo

THE BALLAD OF BABY DOE
257 Willow Song
258 The Silver Aria

MANON
243 Adieu, notre petite table

THE MEDIUM
259 The Black Swan
261 Monica's Waltz

UN BALLO IN MASCHERA
211 Saper vorreste

LA BOHÈME
211 Mi chiamano Mimì
213 Quando men vo
215 Donde lieta

LE NOZZE DI FIGARO
224 Porgi, amor
224 Dove sono i bei momenti
226 Deh vieni, non tardar

CARMEN
237 Je dis que rien ne m'épouvante

I PAGLIACCI
229 Stridono lassù

LES CONTES D'HOFFMANN
239 Elle a fui, la tourterelle!

RIGOLETTO
232 Caro nome

DON GIOVANNI
216 Batti, batti, o bel Masetto
218 Vedrai, carino

ROMÉO ET JULIETTE
245 Ah! Je veux vivre

FALSTAFF
219 Sul fil d'un soffio etesio

DER SCHAUSPIELDIREKTOR
253 Bester Jüngling

FAUST
240 Ah! Je ris de me voir (The Jewel Song)

TARTUFFE
264 Fair Robin I love

FIDELIO
250 O wär' ich schon mit dir vereint

TURANDOT
233 Signore, ascolta!
234 Tu che di gel sei cinta

DER FREISCHÜTZ
251 Kommt ein schlanker Bursch gegangen

DIE ZAUBERFLÖTE
254 Ach, ich fühl's

GIANNI SCHICCHI
220 O mio babbino caro

DICTION COACH
CD TRACK LIST
DISC ONE

		Recitation	Diction Lesson
Arias in Italian			
210	About Italian IPA		
	UN BALLO IN MASCHERA		
211	Saper vorreste	1	2
	LA BOHÈME		
211	Mi chiamano Mimì	3	4
213	Quando men vo	5	6
215	Donde lieta	7	8
	DON GIOVANNI		
216	Batti, batti, o bel Masetto	9	10
218	Vedrai, carino	11	12
	FALSTAFF		
219	Sul fil d'un soffio etesio	13	14
	GIANNI SCHICCHI		
220	O mio babbino caro	15	16
	GIULIO CESARE		
221	V'adoro, pupille	17	18
	MADAMA BUTTERFLY		
221	Un bel dì vedremo	19	20
	LE NOZZE DI FIGARO		
224	Porgi, amor	21	22
224	Dove sono i bei momenti	23	24
226	Deh vieni, non tardar	25	26
	I PAGLIACCI		
229	Stridono lassù	27	28
	RIGOLETTO		
232	Caro nome	29	30
	TURANDOT		
233	Signore, ascolta!	31	32
234	Tu che di gel sei cinta	33	34

DICTION COACH
CD TRACK LIST
DISC TWO

			Recitation	Diction Lesson

Arias in French

	235	About French IPA		
		CARMEN		
	237	Je dis que rien ne m'épouvante	1	2
		LES CONTES D'HOFFMANN		
	239	Elle a fui, la tourterelle!	3	4
		FAUST		
	240	Ah! Je ris de me voir (The Jewel Song)	5	6
		MANON		
	243	Adieu, notre petite table	7	8
		ROMÉO ET JULIETTE		
	245	Ah! Je veux vivre	9	10

Arias in German

	247	About German IPA		
		FIDELIO		
	250	O wär' ich schon mit dir vereint	11	12
		DER FREISCHÜTZ		
	251	Kommt ein schlanker Bursch gegangen	13	14
		DER SCHAUSPIELDIREKTOR		
	253	Bester Jüngling	15	16
		DIE ZAUBERFLÖTE		
	254	Ach, ich fühl's	17	18

Arias in English

	255	About English IPA		
		THE BALLAD OF BABY DOE		
	257	Willow Song	19	20
	258	The Silver Aria	21	22
		THE MEDIUM		
	259	The Black Swan	23	24
	261	Monica's Waltz	25	26
		TARTUFFE		
	264	Fair Robin I love	27	28

ABOUT THE ITALIAN IPA TRANSLITERATIONS
by Martha Gerhart

While the IPA is currently the diction learning tool of choice for singers not familiar with the foreign languages in which they sing, differences in transliterations exist in diction manuals and on the internet, just as differences of pronunciation exist in the Italian language itself.

The Italian transliterations in this volume reflect the following choices:

All unstressed "e's" and "o's" are *closed*. This choice is based on the highest form of the spoken language, as in the authoritative Italian dictionary edited by Zingarelli. However, in practice, singers may well make individual choices as to *closed* or *open* depending upon the vocal tessitura and technical priorities.

Also, there are many Italian words (such as "sento," "cielo," and etc.) for which, in practice, both *closed* and *open* vowels in the *stressed* syllable are perfectly acceptable.

The "nasal 'm'" symbol [ɱ], indicating that the letter "n" assimilates before a "v" or an "f" (such as "inferno" becoming [iɱ ˈfɛr no] in execution, is not used in these transliterations. This choice was a practical one to avoid confusion on the part of the student who might wonder why "in" is transcribed as if it were "im," unlike in any dictionary. However, students are encouraged to use the [ɱ] as advised by experts.

Double consonants which result, in execution, from *phrasal doubling* (*raddoppiamento sintattico*) are not transliterated as such; but students should utilize this sophistication of Italian lyric diction as appropriate.

The syllabic divisions in these transliterations are in the interest of encouraging the singer to lengthen the vowel before a single consonant rather than making an incorrect double consonant, and also to encourage the singer, when there are two consonants, the first of which is *l, m, n,* or *r,* to give more strength to the first of those two consonants.

Intervocalic "s's" are transliterated as *voiced*, despite the fact that in many words ("casa," "così," etc.) the "s" is *unvoiced* in the language (and in the above-mentioned dictionary). Preferred practice for singers is to *voice* those "s's" in the interest of legato; yet, an unvoiced "s" pronunciation in those cases is not incorrect. (*Note*: words which combine a prefix and a stem beginning with an unvoiced "s" ["risolvi," "risanare," etc.] retain the unvoiced "s" of the prefix in singing as well as in speech.)

Many Italian words have alternate pronunciations given in the best dictionaries, particularly regarding closed or open vowels. In my IPA transliterations I chose the first given pronunciation, which is not always the preferred pronunciation in common Italian usage as spoken by Corradina Caporello on the accompanying CDs. I defer to my respected colleague in all cases for her expert pronunciation of beautiful Italian diction.

Pronunciation Key

IPA Symbol	Approximate sound in English	IPA Symbol	Approximate sound in English
[i]	f<u>ee</u>t	[s]	<u>s</u>et
[e]	pot<u>a</u>to	[z]	<u>z</u>ip
[ɛ]	b<u>e</u>d	[l]	<u>l</u>ip
[a]	f<u>a</u>ther	[ʎ]	mi<u>lli</u>on
[ɔ]	t<u>au</u>t		
[o]	t<u>o</u>te	[ɾ]	as *British* "ve<u>r</u>y" – flipped "r"
[u]	t<u>u</u>be	[r]	no English equivalent – rolled "r"
[j]	<u>Y</u>ale		
[w]	<u>w</u>atch	[n]	<u>n</u>ame
		[m]	<u>m</u>op
[b]	<u>b</u>eg	[ŋ]	a<u>n</u>chor
[p]	<u>p</u>et	[ɲ]	o<u>ni</u>on
[d]	<u>d</u>eep	[tʃ]	<u>ch</u>eese
[t]	<u>t</u>op	[dʒ]	<u>G</u>eorge
[g]	<u>G</u>ordon	[dz]	fee<u>ds</u>
[k]	<u>k</u>it	[ts]	fi<u>ts</u>
[v]	<u>v</u>et		
[f]	<u>f</u>it	[ː]	indicates doubled consonants
[ʃ]	<u>sh</u>e	[ˈ]	indicates the primary stress; the syllable following the mark is stressed

UN BALLO IN MASCHERA

music: Giuseppe Verdi

libretto: Antonio Somma (after Eugène Scribe's libretto for Daniel-François Auber's *Gustave III, ou Le Bal Masqué*)

Saper vorreste

sa ˈper   vorː ˈre ste   di   ke   si ˈvɛ ste
Saper   vorreste   di   che   si veste,
to know   you would like   in   what   he is dressed

ˈkwan do   lɛ   ˈkɔ za   ˈke i   vwɔl   na ˈsko za
quando   l'è   cosa   ch'ei   vuol   nascosa.
when   the it is   thing   which he   wants   concealed

ˈɔ skar   lo   sa   ma   nol   di ˈra
Oscar   lo   sa,   ma   nol   dirà.
Oscar   it   knows   but   not it   will tell

tra la la
Tra la la...
tra la la

ˈpjɛ no   da ˈmor   mi   ˈbal tsa   il   kɔr
Pieno   d'amor   mi   balza   il   cor,
full   of love   [in] me   leaps   the   heart

ma   pur   di ˈskre to   ˈsɛr ba   il   se ˈgre to
ma   pur   discreto   serba   il   segreto.
but   yet   discreet   it preserves   the   secret

nol   ra pi ˈra   ˈgra do   o   bel ˈta
Nol   rapirà   grado   o   beltà.
not it   will steal away   rank   or   beauty

tra la la
Tra la la...
tra la la

LA BOHÈME

music: Giacomo Puccini

libretto: Luigi Illica and Giuseppe Giacoso (after the novel *Scènes de la Vie de Bohème* by Henri Murger)

Mi chiamano Mimì

si   mi ˈkja ma no   mi ˈmi
Sì.   Mi chiamano   Mimì,
yes   me they call   Mimì

ma   il   ˈmi o   ˈno me   ɛ   lu ˈtʃi a
ma   il   mio   nome   è   Lucia.
but   the   my   name   is   Lucia

la   ˈstɔ rja   ˈmi a   ɛ   ˈbrɛ ve
La   storia   mia   è   breve:
the   story   mine   is   brief

a   ˈte la   o   a   ˈse ta
A   tela   o   a   seta
on   linen   or   on   silk

ri	ˈka mo	in	ˈka za	e	ˈfwɔ ɾi
ricamo		**in**	**casa**	**e**	**fuori.**
I embroider		*at*	*home*	*and*	*outside*

son	tɾaŋ ˈkwil: la	e	ˈljɛ ta
Son	**tranquilla**	**e**	**lieta,**
I am	*tranquil*	*and*	*happy*

e	ˈdɛ	ˈmi o	ˈzva ɡo	far	ˈdʒiʎ: ʎi	e	ˈrɔ ze
ed	**è**	**mio**	**svago**	**far**	**gigli**	**e**	**rose.**
and	*it is*	*my*	*diversion*	*to make*	*lilies*	*and*	*roses*

mi	ˈpjat: tʃon	ˈkwel: le	ˈkɔ ze
Mi	**piaccion**	**quelle**	**cose**
to me	*are pleasing*	*those*	*things*

ke	an	si	ˈdol tʃe	ma ˈli a
che	**han**	**sì**	**dolce**	**malìa,**
which	*have*	*such*	*sweet*	*charm*

ke	ˈpar la no	da ˈmor	di	pri ma ˈvɛ ɾe
che	**parlano**	**d'amor,**	**di**	**primavere,**
which	*speak*	*of love*	*of*	*springtimes*

ke	ˈpar la no	di	ˈsoɲ: ɲi	e	di	ki ˈmɛ ɾe
che	**parlano**	**di**	**sogni**	**e**	**di**	**chimere—**
which	*speak*	*of*	*dreams*	*and*	*of*	*fantasies*

ˈkwel: le	ˈkɔ ze	ke	an	ˈno me	po e ˈzi a
quelle	**cose**	**che**	**han**	**nome**	**poesia.**
those	*things*	*which*	*have*	*name*	*poetry*

ˈlɛ i	min ˈtɛn de
Lei	**m'intende?**
you	*me understand*

mi	ˈkja ma no	mi ˈmi
Mi	**chiamano**	**Mimì.**
me	*they call*	*Mimì*

il	per ˈke	non sɔ
Il	**perchè**	**non so.**
the	*why*	*not I know*

ˈso la	mi	fɔ	il	ˈpran dzo	da	me	ˈstes: sa
Sola,	**mi**	**fo**	**il**	**pranzo**	**da**	**me**	**stessa.**
alone	*for me*	*I make*	*the*	*lunch/dinner*	*by*	*me*	*myself*

non	ˈva do	ˈsɛm pre	a	ˈmes: sa
Non	**vado**	**sempre**	**a**	**messa**
not	*I go*	*always*	*to*	*mass*

ma	ˈprɛ ɡo	as: ˈsa i	il	siɲ: ˈɲor
ma	**prego**	**assai**	**il**	**Signor.**
but	*I pray [to]*	*much*	*the*	*Lord*

ˈvi vo	ˈso la	so ˈlet: ta
Vivo	**sola,**	**soletta,**
I live	*alone*	*all alone*

la	in	ˈu na	ˈbjaŋ ka	ka me ˈɾet: ta
là	**in**	**una**	**bianca**	**cameretta;**
there	*in*	*a*	*tidy*	*little room*

ˈgwar do	ˈsu i	ˈtetː ti	e	in	ˈtʃɛ lo
guardo	**sui**	**tetti**	**e**	**in**	**cielo.**
I look	*over the*	*rooftops*	*and*	*in*	*sky*

ma	ˈkwan do	vjɛn	lo	ˈzdʒɛ lo
Ma	**quando**	**vien**	**lo**	**sgelo**
but	*when*	*comes*	*the*	*thaw*

il	ˈpri mo	ˈso le	ɛ	ˈmi o
il	**primo**	**sole**	**è**	**mio...**
the	*first*	*sun*	*is*	*mine*

il	ˈpri mo	ˈba tʃo	delː la ˈpri le	ɛ	ˈmi o
il	**primo**	**bacio**	**dell'aprile**	**è**	**mio!**
the	*first*	*kiss*	*of the April*	*is*	*mine*

dʒer ˈmoʎː ʎa	in	un	ˈva zo	ˈu na ˈrɔ za
Germoglia	**in**	**un**	**vaso**	**una rosa...**
blooms	*in*	*a*	*vase*	*a rose*

ˈfɔʎː ʎa	a	ˈfɔʎː ʎa	la ˈspi o
foglia	**a**	**foglia**	**la spio!**
petal	*by*	*petal*	*it I watch*

ko ˈzi	dʒen ˈtil	il	pro ˈfu mo	dun	fjor
Così	**gentil**	**il**	**profumo**	**d'un**	**fior!**
so much	*delicate*	*the*	*perfume*	*of a*	*flower*

ma	i fjor	ˈki o	ˈfatː tʃo	a i ˈmɛ
Ma	**i fior**	**ch'io**	**faccio,**	**ahimè!**
but	*the flowers*	*that I*	*[I] make*	*alas*

non	ˈanː no	o ˈdo ɾe
non	**hanno**	**odore!**
not	*[they] have*	*fragrance*

ˈal tro	di	me	non	le	sa ˈprɛ i
Altro	**di**	**me**	**non**	**le**	**saprei**
other	*of*	*me*	*not*	*to you*	*I would be able*

narː ra ɾe
narrare.
to tell

ˈso no	la	ˈsua	vi ˈtʃi na
Sono	**la**	**sua**	**vicina**
I am	*the*	*your*	*neighbor*

ke	la	vjɛn	ˈfwɔ ɾi ˈdo ɾa	a im por tu ˈna ɾe
che	**la**	**vien**	**fuori d'ora**	**a importunare.**
who	*[her]*	*comes*	*outside of suitable hour*	*to [to] bother*

Quando men vo

ˈkwan do	men	vɔ	so ˈletː ta	per	la ˈvi a
Quando	**men**	**vo**	**soletta**	**per**	**la via**
when	*myself off*	*I go*	*all alone*	*through*	*the street*

la	ˈdʒɛn te	ˈsɔ sta e	ˈmi ɾa
la	**gente**	**sosta e**	**mira...**
the	*people*	*stop and*	*stare*

e	la	bel:ˈlet:tsa	ˈmi a	ˈtut:ta	riˈtʃer ka	in	me
e	**la**	**bellezza**	**mia**	**tutta**	**ricerca**	**in**	**me**
and	*the*	*beauty*	*mine*	*all*	*search*	*in*	*me*

da	ˈka po	a	pjɛ
da	**capo**	**a**	**piè.**
from	*head*	*to*	*foot*

e da:sa ˈpo ro	alˈlor	la	bra mo ˈzi a	sotˈtil
Ed assaporo	**allor**	**la**	**bramosia**	**sottil**
and I savor	*then*	*the*	*longing*	*subtle*

ke	da	ˈʎɔk:ki	traˈspi ra
che	**da**	**gl'occhi**	**traspira;**
which	*from*	*the eyes*	*transpires*

e	ˈda i	pa ˈle zi	ˈvet:tsi	inˈtɛn der	sa
e	**dai**	**palesi**	**vezzi**	**intender**	**sa**
and	*from the*	*revealed*	*charms*	*to understand*	*knows how*

ˈal:le	ok:ˈkul te	belˈta
alle	**occulte**	**beltà.**
to the	*hidden*	*beauty*

koˈzi	lefˈflu vjo	del	deˈzi o
Così	**l'effluvio**	**del**	**desìo**
thus	*the emanation*	*of the*	*desire*

ˈtut:ta	madˈdʒi ra
tutta	**m'aggira;**
completely	*centers around me*

feˈli tʃe	mi	fa
felice	**mi**	**fa!**
happy	*me*	*it makes*

e	tu	ke	ˈsa i	ke mɛˈmo ri
E	**tu**	**che**	**sai,**	**che memori**
and	*you*	*who*	*know*	*who remember*

e	ti ˈstrud:dʒi
e	**ti struggi,**
and	*are pining away*

da	me	ˈtan to	riˈfud:dʒi
da	**me**	**tanto**	**rifuggi?**
from	*me*	*so much*	*you shun*

sɔ	bɛn	le	aŋˈgɔʃ:ʃe	ˈtu e
So	**ben:**	**le**	**angoscie**	**tue**
I know	*well*	*the*	*anguishes*	*your*

non	le	ˈvwɔ i dir
non	**le**	**vuoi dir;**
not	*them*	*you want to say*

sɔ	bɛn
so	**ben,**
I know	*well*

ma	ti ˈsɛn ti	moˈrir
ma	**ti senti**	**morir!**
but	*yourself you feel*	*to die*

Donde lieta

ˈdon de   ˈljɛ ta   uʃːʃi
Donde lieta uscì
from where happy she left

al   ˈtu o   ˈgri do   da ˈmo re
al tuo grido d'amore
at the your cry of love

ˈtor na   ˈso la   mi ˈmi
torna sola Mimì
returns alone Mimi

al   so liˈta rjo   ˈni do
al solitario nido.
to the solitary nest

ri ˈtor na   uˈnal tra   ˈvɔl ta
Ritorna un'altra volta
she goes back another time

a   inˈtɛsːser   ˈfin ti   fjor
a intesser finti fior!
to [to] weave artificial flowers

adːˈdi o   ˈsɛn tsa   raŋˈkor
Addio, senza rancor.
farewell without grudge

aˈskol ta
Ascolta.
listen

le   ˈpɔ ke   ˈrɔ be   aˈdu na
Le poche robe aduna
the few things collect

ke   laʃːˈʃa i   ˈspar se
che lasciai sparse.
which I left strewn here and there

nel   ˈmi o   kasːˈsetːto   stan   ˈkju zi
Nel mio cassetto stan chiusi
in the my drawer are shut

kwel   tʃerˈkjetːto   dɔr
quel cerchietto d'or,
that little ring of gold

e   il   ˈli bro   di   preˈgjɛ re
e il libro di preghiere.
and the book of prayers

inˈvɔl dʒi   ˈtutːto ˈkwan to   in   un   gremˈbja le
Involgi tutto quanto in un grembiale
wrap up all that in an apron

e   man deˈrɔ   il   porˈtjɛ re
e manderò il portiere...
and I will send the porter

ˈba da   ˈsotːto   il   gwanˈtʃa le
Bada... sotto il guanciale
be careful under the pillow

tʃɛ	la	kufˈfjet: ta	ˈrɔ za
c'è	**la**	**cuffietta**	**rosa.**
there is	*the*	*bonnet*	*pink*

se	ˈvwɔ i
Se	**vuoi,**
if	*you wish*

serˈbar la	a	riˈkɔr do	daˈmor
serbarla	**a**	**ricordo**	**d'amor!**
preserve it	*in*	*remembrance*	*of love*

adˈdi o	ˈsɛn tsa	raŋˈkor
Addio,	**senza**	**rancor.**
farewell	*without*	*grudge*

DON GIOVANNI

music: Wolfgang Amadeus Mozart
libretto: Lorenzo da Ponte (after Giovanni Bertati's libretto for Giuseppe Gazzaniga's *Il convitato di pietra*; also after the Don Juan legends)

Batti, batti, o bel Masetto

ma	se	ˈkol pa	ˈi o	non	ɔ
Ma	**se**	**colpa**	**io**	**non**	**ho!**
but	*if*	*fault*	*I*	*not*	*I have*

ma	se	da	ˈlu i	iŋ ganˈna ta	riˈma zi
Ma	**se**	**da**	**lui**	**ingannata**	**rimasi…**
but	*if*	*by*	*him*	*deceived*	*I remained*

e	ˈpɔ i	ke	ˈtɛ mi
E	**poi**	**che**	**temi?**
and	*then*	*what*	*you fear*

traŋˈkwil: la ti	ˈmi a	ˈvi ta
Tranquillati,	**mia**	**vita:**
reassure yourself	*my*	*life*

non	mi	tokˈkɔ	la	ˈpun ta	ˈdel: le	ˈdi ta
non	**mi**	**toccò**	**la**	**punta**	**delle**	**dita.**
not	*to me*	*he touched*	*the*	*tip*	*of the*	*fingers*

non	me	lo	ˈkre di
Non	**me**	**lo**	**credi?**
not	*me*	*it*	*you believe*

iŋˈgra to
Ingrato!
ungrateful

vjɛn	kwi	ˈsfo ga ti	amˈmat: tsa mi
Vien	**qui,**	**sfogati,**	**ammazzami—**
come	*here*	*vent [your anger]*	*kill me*

fa	ˈtut: to	di	me	kwel	ke	ti	ˈpja tʃe
fa'	**tutto**	**di**	**me**	**quel**	**che**	**ti**	**piace;**
do	*everything*	*with*	*me*	*that*	*which*	*you*	*pleases*

ma	ˈpɔ i	maˈzet: to	ˈmi o
ma	**poi,**	**Masetto**	**mio,**
but	*afterwards*	*Masetto*	*mine*

fa   'pa tʃe
fa'   pace.
make   peace

'bat: ti   o   bɛl   ma 'zet: to
Batti,   o   bel   Masetto,
beat   o   handsome   Masetto

la   'tu a   'pɔ ve ɾa   dzer 'li na
la   tua   povera   Zerlina.
the   your   poor   Zerlina

sta 'ɾɔ   kwi   'ko me   aɲ: ɲel: 'li na
Starò   qui   come   agnellina
I will stay   here   like   little lamb

le   'tue   'bɔt: te   a da spet: 'tar
le   tue   botte   ad aspettar.
the   your   blows   to await

laʃ: ʃe 'ɾɔ   strat: 'tsjar mi   il   'kri ne
Lascerò   straziarmi   il   crine,
I will let   to tear out [of] me   the   head of hair

laʃ: ʃe 'ɾɔ   ka 'var mi   ʎi   'ɔk: ki
lascerò   cavarmi   gli   occhi,
I will let   to pull out [of] me   the   eyes

e   le   'ka ɾe   'tu e   ma 'ni ne   'ljɛ ta   'pɔ i
e   le   care   tue   manine   lieta   poi
and   the   beloved   your   dear hands   happy   then

sa 'pɾɔ   ba 'tʃar
saprò   baciar.
I will be able   to kiss

a   lo   've do   non   'a i   'kɔ ɾe
Ah,   lo   vedo,   non   hai   core:
ah   it   I see   not   you have   heart

'pa tʃe   o   'vi ta   'mi a
Pace,   o   vita   mia;
peace   o   life   mine

iŋ kon 'tɛn ti   e dal: le 'gri a
in contenti   ed allegria
in   contentments   and cheerfulness

'nɔt: te   e   di   voʎ: 'ʎam   pas: 'sar
notte   e   dì   vogliam   passar,
night   and   day   let us wish   to pass

si   si
sì   sì...
yes   yes

Vedrai, carino

ve	ˈdra i		ka ˈri no
Vedrai,			**carino,**
you will see			*dear one*

se	ˈsɛ i		bwo ˈni no
se	**sei**		**buonino,**
if	*you are*		*good*

ke	bɛl		ri ˈmɛ djo
che	**bel**		**rimedio**
what	*beautiful*		*remedy*

ti	ˈvoʎ: ʎo		dar
ti	**voglio**		**dar.**
to you	*I want*		*to give*

ɛ	na tu ˈra le
È	**naturale,**
it is	*natural*

non	da	diz ˈgu sto
non	**da**	**disgusto,**
not	*it gives*	*bad taste*

e	lo	spet: ˈtsja le
e	**lo**	**speziale**
and	*the*	*pharmacist*

non	lo	sa	far
non	**lo**	**sa**	**far,**
not	*it*	*knows how*	*to make*

nɔ	non	lo	sa	far
no,	**non**	**lo**	**sa**	**far.**
no	*not*	*it*	*knows how*	*to make*

ɛ	un	ˈtʃɛr to	ˈbal sa mo
È	**un**	**certo**	**balsamo**
it is	*a*	*certain*	*balm*

ke	ˈpɔr to	ad: ˈdɔs: so
che	**porto**	**addosso.**
that	*I carry*	*on me*

ˈda ɾe	tel	ˈpɔs: so
Dare	**te'l**	**posso,**
to give	*to you it*	*I can*

sel	ˈvwɔ i	pro ˈvar
se'l	**vuoi**	**provar.**
if it	*you want*	*to try*

sa ˈper	vor: ˈre sti
Saper	**vorresti**
to know	*you would want*

ˈdo ve	mi	sta
dove	**mi**	**sta?**
where	*[on] me*	*it is*

ˈsɛn ti lo	ˈbat: te ɾe
Sentilo	**battere,**
feel it	*to beat*

ˈtok: ka mi	kwa
toccami	**qua.**
touch me	*here*

FALSTAFF

music: Giuseppe Verdi
libretto: Arrigo Boito (after plays by William Shakespeare, *The Merry Wives of Windsor* and *Henry IV*)

Sul fil d'un soffio etesio

sul	fil	dun	ˈsofː fjo	e ˈtɛ zi o
Sul	**fil**	**d'un**	**soffio**	**etesio**
upon the	*thread*	*of a*	*breath*	*etesian*

skorː ˈre te	ˈa dʒi li	ˈlar ve
scorrete,	**agili**	**larve;**
fly	*agile*	*shadows*

fra	i	ˈra mi	un	baʎː ˈʎor	ˈtʃe zi o
fra	**i**	**rami**	**un**	**baglior**	**cesio**
among	*the*	*branches*	*a*	*flash*	*bluish*

ˈdal ba	lu ˈna ɾe	apː ˈpar ve
d'alba	**lunare**	**apparve.**
of dawning	*lunar*	*[has] appeared*

dan ˈtsa te	e	il	ˈpasː so	ˈblan do
Danzate!	**E**	**il**	**passo**	**blando**
dance	*and*	*the*	*step*	*soft*

mi ˈzu ɾi	un	ˈblan do	swɔn
misuri	**un**	**blando**	**suon,**
let measure	*a*	*gentle*	*sound*

le	ˈma dʒi ke	akː kopː ˈpjan do	ka ˈrɔ le
le	**magiche**	**accoppiando**	**carole**
the	*magical*	*combining*	*dances*

ˈalː la	kan ˈtson
alla	**canzon.**
to the	*song*

erː ˈrjam	ˈsotː to	la	ˈlu na
Erriam	**sotto**	**la**	**luna**
let us wander	*beneath*	*the*	*moon*

ʃeʎː ˈʎɛn do	fjor	da	ˈfjo ɾe
scegliendo	**fior**	**da**	**fiore;**
choosing	*flower*	*by*	*flower*

ˈoɲː ɲi	ko ˈrɔlː la	iŋ	ˈkɔ ɾe
ogni	**corolla**	**in**	**core**
every	*corolla*	*in*	*heart*

ˈpɔr ta	la	ˈsu a	for ˈtu na
porta	**la**	**sua**	**fortuna.**
brings	*the*	*its*	*[good] luck*

ˈko i	ˈdʒiʎː ʎi	e	le	ˈvi ɔ le
Coi	**gigli**	**e**	**le**	**vïole**
with the	*lilies*	*and*	*the*	*violets*

skri ˈvjam	de	ˈno mi	ar ˈka ni
scriviam	**de'**	**nomi**	**arcani;**
let us write	*of*	*names*	*secret*

ˈdalː le	fa ˈta te	ˈma ni
dalle	**fatate**	**mani**
from the	*enchanted*	*hands*

dʒer	'moʎ:	ʎi no	pa 'rɔ le		
germoglino			**parole...**		
let bloom			*words*		

pa 'rɔ le	al: lu mi 'na te	di	'pu ro	ar 'dʒɛn to
parole	**alluminate**	**di**	**puro**	**argento**
words	*illuminated*	*with*	*pure*	*silver*

e	dɔr
e	**d'or...**
and	*with gold...*

'kar mi	e	ma 'li e
carmi	**e**	**malìe.**
magical words	*and*	*charms*

le	'fa te	'an: no	per	'tʃi fre
Le	**Fate**	**hanno**	**per**	**cifre**
the	*fairies*	*have*	*for*	*ciphers*

i	fjor
i	**fior.**
the	*flowers*

GIANNI SCHICCHI

music: Giacomo Puccini
libretto: Giovacchino Foranzo (based on an episode in Dante's *Inferno*)

O mio babbino caro

o	'mi o	bab: 'bi no	'ka ro
O	**mio**	**babbino**	**caro,**
oh	*my*	*daddy*	*dear*

mi	'pja tʃe,	ɛ	'bɛl: lo
mi	**piace,**	**è**	**bello;**
me	*he pleases*	*he is*	*handsome*

vɔ	an 'da re	in	'pɔr ta	'ros: sa
vo'	**andare**	**in**	**Porta**	**Rossa**
I want	*to go*	*to*	*Porta*	*Rossa*

a	kom pe 'rar	la 'nɛl: lo
a	**comperar**	**l'anello!**
to	*[to] buy*	*the ring*

si	tʃi	'vɔʎ: ʎo	an 'da re
Sì,	**ci**	**voglio**	**andare!**
yes	*there*	*I want*	*to go*

e	se	la 'mas: si	in 'dar no
E	**se**	**l'amassi**	**indarno,**
and	*if*	*him I should have loved*	*in vain*

an 'drɛ i	sul	'pon te	'vɛk: kjo
andrei	**sul**	**Ponte**	**Vecchio,**
I should go	*to the*	*Ponte*	*Vecchio*

ma	per	but: 'tar mi	in	'ar no
ma	**per**	**buttarmi**	**in**	**Arno!**
but	*for*	*to throw myself*	*into*	*Arno*

mi	'strug: go	e	mi tor 'men to
Mi	**struggo**	**e**	**mi tormento!**
I am consumed [with desire]		*and*	*I am tormented*

o	ˈdi o	vorː ˈrɛ i	mo ˈrir
O	**Dio,**	**vorrei**	**morir!**
Oh	*God*	*I should like*	*to die*

ˈbabː bo	pje ˈta
Babbo,	**pietà!**
Daddy	*[have] pity*

GIULIO CESARE
music: George Frideric Handel
libretto: Nicola Francesco Haym (after history and legend)

V'adoro, pupille

va ˈdo ro	pu ˈpilː le
V'adoro,	**pupille,**
you I adore	*eyes*

sa ˈetː te	da ˈmo re
saette	**d'amore;**
darts	*of love*

le	ˈvɔ stre	fa ˈvilː le
le	**vostre**	**faville**
the	*your*	*sparks*

son	ˈɡra te	nel	sen
son	**grate**	**nel**	**sen.**
are	*welcome*	*in the*	*breast*

pje ˈto ze	vi	ˈbra ma
Pietose	**vi**	**brama**
compassionate	*you*	*longs for*

il	ˈmɛ sto	ˈmi o	ˈkɔ re
il	**mesto**	**mio**	**core,**
the	*sad*	*my*	*heart*

koɲː ˈɲo ra	vi ˈkja ma
ch'ogn'ora	**vi chiama**
which [in] every hour	*you calls*

la ˈma to	ˈsu o	bɛn
l'amato	**suo**	**ben.**
the beloved	*its*	*dear one*

MADAMA BUTTERFLY
music: Giacomo Puccini
libretto: Luigi Illica and Giuseppe Giacoso (after the play by David Belasco, which was based on a story by John Luther Long)

Un bel dì vedremo

ˈpjan dʒi	per ˈke
Piangi?	**Perchè?**
you weep	*why*

a	la	ˈfe de	ti	ˈmaŋ ka
Ah,	**la**	**fede**	**ti**	**manca!**
ah	*the*	*faith*	*in you*	*is lacking*

ˈsɛn ti
Senti.
listen

un	bɛl	di	ve ˈdre mo	
Un	**bel**	**dì**	**vedremo**	
one	*beautiful*	*day*	*we shall see*	

le ˈvar si	un	fil	di	ˈfu mo
levarsi	**un**	**fil**	**di**	**fumo**
to rise	*a*	*thread*	*of*	*smoke*

sul: le ˈstrɛ mo	kon ˈfin	del	ˈma ɾe
sull'estremo	**confin**	**del**	**mare.**
over the far	*boundry*	*of the*	*sea*

e	ˈpɔ i	la	ˈna ve ap: ˈpa ɾe
E	**poi**	**la**	**nave appare.**
and	*then*	*the*	*ship appears*

ˈpɔ i	la	ˈna ve	ˈbjaŋ ka	ˈen tra nel	ˈpɔr to
Poi	**la**	**nave**	**bianca**	**entra nel**	**porto,**
then	*the*	*ship*	*white*	*enters in the*	*port*

ˈrom ba	il	ˈsu o sa ˈlu to
romba	**il**	**suo saluto.**
roars	*the*	*its salutation*

ˈve di	ɛ	ve ˈnu to
Vedi?	**È**	**venuto**
you see	*he is*	*arrived*

ˈi o	non	ʎi	ˈʃen do iŋ ˈkon tro	ˈi o	nɔ
Io	**non**	**gli**	**scendo incontro —**	**io**	**no.**
I	*not*	*him*	*[I] go down toward*	*I*	*no*

mi	ˈmet: to	la
Mi	**metto**	**là**
myself	*I put*	*there*

sul	ˈtʃiʎ: ʎo	del	ˈkɔl: le
sul	**ciglio**	**del**	**colle**
on the	*edge*	*of the*	*hill*

e	a ˈspɛt: to	gran	ˈtɛm po
e	**aspetto**	**gran**	**tempo;**
and	*I wait*	*great*	*length of time*

e	non	mi	ˈpe za
e	**non**	**mi**	**pesa,**
and	*not*	*me*	*it burdens*

la	ˈluŋ ga	at: ˈte za
la	**lunga**	**attesa.**
the	*long*	*wait*

e	uʃ: ˈʃi to	ˈdal: la	ˈfol: la	tʃit: ta ˈdi na
E...	**uscito**	**dalla**	**folla**	**cittadina**
and	*come out*	*from the*	*crowd*	*town*

un	ˈwɔ mo	un	ˈpit: tʃol	ˈpun to
un	**uomo,**	**un**	**picciol**	**punto**
a	*man*	*a*	*little*	*dot*

sav: ˈvi a	per	la	kol: ˈli na
s'avvia	**per**	**la**	**collina.**
starts off	*for*	*the*	*hill*

ki sa ˈra
Chi sarà?
who it will be

e ˈko me sa ˈra ˈdʒun to
E come sarà giunto
and as soon as he will be arrived

ke di ˈra
che dirà?
what he will say

kja me ˈra batː tɛr ˈfla i ˈdalː la lon ˈta na
Chiamerà Butterfly dalla lontana.
he will call Butterfly from the distance

ˈi o ˈsɛn tsa dar ri ˈspo sta
Io senza dar risposta
I without to give response

me ne sta ˈrɔ na ˈsko sta
me ne starò nascosta
me from him I shall be hidden

un pɔ per ˈʃɛ lja
un po' per celia
a little for jest

e un pɔ per non mo ˈri ɾe
e un po' per non morire
and a little for not to die

al ˈpri mo iŋ ˈkon tro
al primo incontro.
at the first encounter

e ˈdeʎː ʎi al ˈkwan to in ˈpe na kja me ˈra
Ed egli alquanto in pena chiamerà:
and he somewhat in suffering will call

pitː ˈtʃi na moʎː ʎe ˈti na
Piccina mogliettina,
little dear wife

o ˈledː dzo di ver ˈbɛ na
olezzo di verbena,
fragrance of verbena

i ˈno mi ke mi ˈda va al ˈsu o ve ˈni ɾe
i nomi che mi dava al suo venire.
the names which me he gave at the his coming

ˈtutː to ˈkwe sto avː verː ˈra te lo pro ˈmetː to
Tutto questo avverrà, te lo prometto.
all this will happen you it I promise

ˈtjɛn ti la ˈtu a pa ˈu ɾa
Tienti la tua paura;
hold onto the your fear

ˈi o kon si ˈku ɾa ˈfe de la ˈspɛtː to
io con sicura fede l'aspetto.
I with sure faith him I await

LE NOZZE DI FIGARO

music: Wolfgang Amadeus Mozart
libretto: Lorenzo da Ponte (after *La Folle Journée, ou Le Mariage de Figaro,* a comedy by Pierre Augustin Caron de Beaumarchais)

Porgi, amor

ˈpɔr dʒi   a ˈmor
Porgi,   amor,
offer   love

ˈkwal ke   ri ˈstɔ ɾo
qualche   ristoro
some   relief

al   ˈmi o   ˈdwɔ lo
al   mio   duolo,
to the   my   sorrow

a   ˈmjɛ i   so ˈspir
a'   miei   sospir!
to [the]   my   sighs

o   mi   ˈrɛn di
O   mi   rendi
either   to me   give back

il   ˈmi o   te ˈzɔ ɾo
il   mio   tesoro,
the   my   treasure

o   mi   ˈlaʃ: ʃa   al ˈmen
o   mi   lascia   almen
or   me   let   at least

mo ˈrir
morir!
[to] die

Dove sono i bei momenti

e   su ˈzan: na   non   vjɛn
E   Susanna   non   vien!
and   Susanna   not   comes

ˈso no   an ˈsjo za   di   sa ˈper   ˈko me   il   ˈkon te
Sono   ansiosa   di   saper   come   il   Conte
I am   anxious   of   to know   how   the   Count

ak: ˈkɔl se   la   pro ˈpo sta
accolse   la   proposta.
welcomed   the   proposal

al ˈkwan to   ar ˈdi to   il   pro ˈdʒɛt: to   mi   par
Alquanto   ardito   il   progetto   mi   par,
rather   bold   the   project   to me   seems

e   a ˈdu no   ˈspɔ zo   si   vi ˈva tʃe
e   ad uno   sposo   sì   vivace
and   to a   husband   so   spirited

e   dʒe ˈlo zo
e   geloso!
and   jealous

ma	ke	mal	tʃɛ
Ma	**che**	**mal**	**c'è?**
but	*what*	*harm*	*there is*

kan	'dʒan do	i	'mjɛ i	ve 'sti ti
cangiando		**i**	**miei**	**vestiti**
changing		*the*	*my*	*clothes*

kon	'kwel: li	di	su 'zan: na
con	**quelli**	**di**	**Susanna,**
with	*those*	*of*	*Susanna*

e	i	'swɔ i	co	'mjɛ i
e	**i**	**suoi**	**co'**	**miei**
and	*the*	*hers*	*with [the]*	*mine*

al	fa 'vor	'del: la	'nɔt: te
al	**favor**	**della**	**notte.**
at the	*favor*	*of the*	*night*

o	'tʃɛ lo
Oh	**cielo!**
oh	*heaven*

a	kwal	'u mil	'sta to	fa 'ta le
A	**qual**	**umil**	**stato**	**fatale**
to	*what*	*humble*	*state*	*unfortunate*

'i o	son	ri 'dɔt: ta	da	un	kon 'sɔr te	kru 'dɛl
io	**son**	**ridotta**	**da**	**un**	**consorte**	**crudel!**
I	*am*	*reduced*	*by*	*a*	*husband*	*cruel*

ke	'do po	a 'ver mi	kon	un	'mi sto	i na u 'di to
che	**dopo**	**avermi**	**con**	**un**	**misto**	**inaudito**
who	*after*	*having me*	*with*	*a*	*mixture*	*incredible*

din fe del 'ta	di	dʒe lo 'zi a	di	'zdeɲ: ɲo
d'infedeltà,	**di**	**gelosia,**	**di**	**sdegno!**
of infedelity	*of*	*jealousy*	*of*	*disdain*

'pri ma	a 'ma ta
prima	**amata,**
first	*loved*

'in di	of: 'fe za
indi	**offesa,**
then	*offended*

e	al 'fin	tra 'di ta
e	**alfin**	**tradita,**
and	*finally*	*betrayed*

'fam: mi	or	tʃer 'kar
fammi	**or**	**cercar**
makes me	*now*	*to seek*

da	'u na	'mi a	'sɛr va	a 'i ta
da	**una**	**mia**	**serva**	**aita!**
from	*a*	*my*	*servant*	*help*

ˈdo ve	ˈso no	i	ˈbɛ i	mo ˈmen ti	
Dove	**sono**	**i**	**bei**	**momenti**	
where	*are*	*the*	*beautiful*	*moments*	

di	dol ˈtʃet: tsa	e	di	pja ˈtʃer
di	**dolcezza**	**e**	**di**	**piacer?**
of	*sweetness*	*and*	*of*	*pleasure*

ˈdo ve	an ˈda ɾo	i	dʒu ɾa ˈmen ti	
Dove	**andaro**	**i**	**giuramenti**	
where	*went*	*the*	*promises*	

di	kwel	ˈlab: bro	men tsoɲ: ˈɲer
di	**quel**	**labbro**	**menzogner?**
of	*that*	*lip*	*lying*

per ˈke	ˈma i	se	in	ˈpjan ti	e in ˈpe ne
Perchè	**mai,**	**se**	**in**	**pianti**	**e in pene**
why	*ever*	*if*	*in*	*tears*	*and in sufferings*

per me	ˈtut: to	si kan ˈdʒɔ	
per me	**tutto**	**si cangiò,**	
for me	*everything*	*changed*	

la	me ˈmɔ ɾja	di	kwel	ˈbɛ ne
la	**memoria**	**di**	**quel**	**bene**
the	*memory*	*of*	*that*	*dear one*

dal	ˈmi o	sen	non	tra pas: ˈsɔ
dal	**mio**	**sen**	**non**	**trapassò?**
from the	*my*	*breast*	*not*	*[has] left*

a	se	al ˈmen	la	ˈmi a ko ˈstan tsa
Ah!	**se**	**almen**	**la**	**mia costanza**
ah	*if*	*at least*	*the*	*my constancy*

nel	laŋ ˈgwi ɾe	a ˈman do	oɲ: ˈɲor
nel	**languire**	**amando**	**ognor**
in the	*languishing*	*loving*	*always*

mi	por ˈtas: se	ˈu na	spe ˈɾan tsa
mi	**portasse**	**una**	**speranza**
to me	*may bring*	*a*	*hope*

di	kan ˈdʒar	liŋ ˈgra to	kɔr
di	**cangiar**	**l'ingrato**	**cor.**
of	*changing*	*the ungrateful*	*heart*

Deh vieni, non tardar

ˈdʒun se	al ˈfin	il	mo ˈmen to
Giunse	**alfin**	**il**	**momento**
arrives	*finally*	*the*	*moment*

ke	go ˈdrɔ	ˈsen tsa	af: ˈfan: no
che	**godrò**	**senza**	**affanno**
which	*I will enjoy*	*without*	*anxiety*

in	ˈbrat: tʃo	al: ˈli dol	ˈmi o
in	**braccio**	**all'idol**	**mio.**
in	*arm*	*of the idol*	*mine*

'ti mi de	'ku ɾe
Timide	**cure!**
timid	*cares*

uʃː	'ʃi te	dal	'mi o	'pɛtː to
	uscite	**dal**	**mio**	**petto;**
	go out	*from the*	*my*	*breast*

a	tur 'bar	non	ve 'ni te
a	**turbar**	**non**	**venite**
to	*[to] disturb*	*not*	*come*

il	'mi o	di 'lɛtː to
il	**mio**	**diletto!**
the	*my*	*pleasure*

o	'ko me	par
Oh	**come**	**par**
oh	*how*	*it seems*

ke	alː la mo 'ro zo	'fɔ ko
che	**all'amoroso**	**foco**
that	*to the amorous*	*fire*

la me ni 'ta	del	'lɔ ko
l'amenità	**del**	**loco,**
the pleasantness	*of the*	*place*

la	'tɛrː ra	e	il	tʃɛl
la	**terra**	**e**	**il**	**ciel**
the	*earth*	*and*	*the*	*sky*

ri 'spon da
risponda,
respond

'ko me	la	'nɔtː te
come	**la**	**notte**
as	*the*	*night*

i	'fur ti	'mjɛ i	se 'kon da
i	**furti**	**miei**	**seconda!**
the	*deceits*	*mine*	*favors*

dɛ	'vjɛ ni
Deh	**vieni,**
please	*come*

non	tar 'dar	o	'dʒɔ ja	'bɛlː la
non	**tardar,**	**o**	**gioja**	**bella.**
not	*to delay*	*oh*	*joy*	*beautiful*

'vjɛ ni	'o ve	a 'mo ɾe
Vieni	**ove**	**amore**
come	*where*	*love*

per	go 'der	tapː 'pɛlː la
per	**goder**	**t'appella**
for	*to enjoy*	*you calls*

fiŋ 'ke	non	'splɛn de	in	tʃɛl
finchè	**non**	**splende**	**in**	**ciel**
until	*not*	*shines*	*in*	*sky*

noˈtːurna	ˈtur na	ˈfa tʃe	
notturna		**face–**	
noctural		*torch*	

fiŋ ˈke	ˈla rja	ɛ	aŋ ˈkor	ˈbru na
finchè	**l'aria**	**è**	**ancor**	**bruna,**
until	*the air*	*is*	*again*	*dark*

e	il	ˈmon do	ˈta tʃe
e	**il**	**mondo**	**tace.**
and	*the*	*world*	*is silent*

kwi	ˈmor mo ra	il	ruʃː ˈʃɛl
Qui	**mormora**	**il**	**ruscel,**
here	*murmurs*	*the*	*stream*

kwi	ˈsker tsa	ˈla u ra
qui	**scherza**	**l'aura,**
here	*plays*	*the breeze*

ke	kol	ˈdol tʃe	su ˈsurː ro
che	**col**	**dolce**	**susurro**
which	*with the*	*gentle*	*rustling*

il	kɔr	ri ˈsta u ra
il	**cor**	**ristaura,**
the	*heart*	*revives*

kwi	ˈri do no	i	fjo ˈretː ti
qui	**ridono**	**i**	**fioretti**
here	*laugh*	*the*	*little flowers*

e	ˈlɛr ba	ɛ	ˈfre ska
e	**l'erba**	**è**	**fresca.**
and	*the grass*	*is*	*fresh*

ˈa i	pja ˈtʃe ri	da ˈmor
Ai	**piaceri**	**d'amor**
to the	*pleasures*	*of love*

kwi	ˈtutː to	a ˈde ska
qui	**tutto**	**adesca.**
here	*everything*	*lures*

ˈvjɛ ni	bɛn	ˈmi o
Vieni,	**ben**	**mio,**
come	*dear one*	*mine*

tra	ˈkwe ste	ˈpjan te	a ˈsko ze
tra	**queste**	**piante**	**ascose!**
among	*these*	*trees*	*hidden from view*

ti	vɔ	la	ˈfron te	iŋ ko ro ˈnar
Ti	**vo'**	**la**	**fronte**	**incoronar**
to you	*I want*	*the*	*forehead*	*to crown*

di	ˈrɔ ze
di	**rose.**
with	*roses*

I PAGLIACCI
music: Ruggero Leoncavallo
libretto: Ruggero Leoncavallo (based on a legal case his father heard as a judge)

Stridono lassù
(Ballatella)

kwal	ˈfjam: ma	a ˈve a	nel	ˈgwar do
Qual	**fiamma**	**avea**	**nel**	**guardo!**
what	*fire*	*he had*	*in the*	*look*

ʎi	ˈɔk: ki	ab: bas: ˈsa i
Gli	**occhi**	**abbassai**
the	*eyes*	*I lowered*

per	ˈtɛ ma	ˈke i	led: ˈdʒes: se
per	**tema**	**ch'ei**	**leggesse**
for	*fear*	*that he*	*may have read*

il	ˈmi o	pen ˈsjɛr	se ˈgre to
il	**mio**	**pensier**	**segreto!**
the	*my*	*thought*	*secret*

o	ˈse i	mi	sor pren ˈdes: se
Oh!	**s'ei**	**mi**	**sorprendesse...**
oh	*if he*	*me*	*should take by surprise*

bru ˈta le	ˈko me	ˈeʎ: ʎi	ɛ
brutale	**come**	**egli**	**è!**
brutish	*as*	*he*	*is*

ma	ˈba sti	or	ˈvi a
Ma	**basti,**	**or**	**via.**
but	*suffice it*	*now*	*away*

son	ˈkwe sti	ˈsoɲ: ɲi	pa u ˈro zi	e	ˈfɔ le
Son	**questi**	**sogni**	**paurosi**	**e**	**fole!**
are	*these*	*dreams*	*frightful*	*and*	*fairy tales*

o	ke	bɛl	ˈso le	di	mɛd: dza ˈgo sto
O	**che**	**bel**	**sole**	**di**	**mezz'agosto!**
oh	*what*	*beautiful*	*sun*	*of*	*middle August*

ˈi o	son	ˈpjɛ na	di	ˈvi ta	e
Io	**son**	**piena**	**di**	**vita,**	**e,**
I	*am*	*full*	*of*	*life*	*and*

ˈtut: ta	il: laŋ gwi ˈdi ta	per	ar ˈka no	de ˈzi o
tutta	**illanguidita**	**per**	**arcano**	**desìo,**
completely	*become weakened*	*through*	*secret*	*desire*

non	sɔ	ke	ˈbra mo
non	**so**	**che**	**bramo!**
not	*I know*	*what*	*I long for*

o	ke	ˈvo lo	da u ˈdʒel: li
Oh!	**che**	**volo**	**d'augelli,**
oh	*what*	*flight*	*of birds*

e	ˈkwan te	ˈstri da
e	**quante**	**strida!**
and	*how much*	*shrilling [bird] cries*

ke	ˈkjɛ don	ˈdo ve	van
Che	**chiedon?**	**Dove**	**van?**
what	*they ask for*	*where*	*they go*

kis: 'sa
Chissà?
who knows

la 'mam: ma 'mi a
La mamma mia,
the mama mine

ke la 'bwɔ na ven 'tu ɾa an: nun 'tsja va
che la buona ventura annunziava,
who the good fortune predicted

kom pren 'de va il lor 'kan to
comprendeva il lor canto,
understood the their singing

e a me bam 'bi na ko 'zi kan 'ta va
e a me bambina così cantava:
and to me child thus sang

'u i
Hui!
Ah

'stri do no las 'su li be ɾa 'men te
Stridono lassù, liberamente
they chirp up above freely

lan 'tʃa ti a vol 'ko me 'fret: tʃe
lanciati a vol come frecce,
launched in flight like arrows

ʎi a u 'dʒɛl
gli augel.
the birds

di 'sfi da no le 'nu bi
Disfidano le nubi
they defy the clouds

el sol ko 'tʃɛn te
e'l sol cocente,
and the sun burning

e 'van: no per le 'vi e del tʃɛl
e vanno per le vie del ciel.
and they go through the paths of the heaven

laʃ: 'ʃa te li va 'gar per lat mo 'sfɛ ɾa
Lasciateli vagar per l'atmosfera,
let them [to] roam through the atmosphere

'kwe sti as: se 'ta ti dad: 'dzur: ro
questi assetati d'azzurro
these [ones] thirsty for blue [sky]

e di splen 'dor
e di splendor:
and for splendor

'se gwo no aŋ 'kes: si un 'soɲ: ɲo
seguono anch'essi un sogno,
they follow also they a dream

IPA	Italian	English
'u na ki 'mɛ ɾa	**una chimera,**	*a fantasy*
e 'van: no fra le 'nu bi dɔr	**e vanno fra le nubi d'or!**	*and they go among the clouds of gold*
ke iŋ 'kal tsi il 'vɛn to	**Che incalzi il vento**	*that may rise the wind*
e 'la tri la tem 'pɛ sta	**e latri la tempesta,**	*and may howl the tempest*
kon 'la li a 'pɛr te	**con l'ali aperte**	*with the wings open*
san 'tut: to sfi 'dar	**san tutto sfidar;**	*they know how everything to defy*
la 'pjɔd: dʒa i 'lam pi 'nul: la 'ma i	**la pioggia, i lampi — nulla mai**	*the rain the lightning nothing ever*
li ar: 'rɛ sta	**li arresta,**	*them stops*
e 'van: no 'suʎ: ʎi a 'bis: si e i mar	**e vanno sugli abissi e i mar.**	*and they go over the chasms and the seas*
'van: no lad: 'dʒu 'vɛr so un pa 'e ze 'stra no	**Vanno laggiù verso un paese strano**	*they go down there toward a land strange*
ke 'soɲ: ɲan 'for se	**che sognan forse**	*which they dream of perhaps*
e ke 'tʃer ka no in van	**e che cercano in van.**	*and which they search for in vain*
ma i bo 'ɛ mi del tʃɛl	**Ma i boëmi del ciel**	*but the bohemians of the sky*
'se gwon lar 'ka no po 'ter	**seguon l'arcano poter**	*follow the mysterious power*
ke li so 'spin dʒe	**che li sospinge...**	*which them propels*
e van	**e van!**	*and they go*

RIGOLETTO

music: Giuseppe Verdi
libretto: Francesco Maria Piave (after Victor Hugo's drama *Le Roi s'Amuse*)

Caro nome

gwal ˈtjɛr   mal ˈde
Gualtier   Maldè!
Walter   Maldè

ˈno me   di   ˈlu i   si   a ˈma to
nome   di   lui   sì   amato,
name   of   him   so much   loved

ti   skol ˈpiʃː ʃi
ti   scolpisci
yourself   you engrave

nel   ˈkɔ re   inː na mo ˈra to
nel   core   innamorato!
in the   heart   enamored

ˈka ro   ˈno me   ke   il   ˈmi o   kɔr
Caro   nome   che   il   mio   cor
dear   name   which   the   my   heart

ˈfe sti   ˈpri mo   pal pi ˈtar
festi   primo   palpitar,
made   first   to palpitate

le   de ˈlit: tsje   delː la ˈmor
le   delizie   dell'amor
the   delights   of the love

mi   ˈdɛ i   ˈsɛm pre   ramː men ˈtar
mi   dêi   sempre   rammentar!
to me   you must   always   [to] recall

kol   pen ˈsjɛr   il   ˈmi o   de ˈzir
Col   pensier   il   mio   desir
with the   thought   the   my   desire

a   te   ˈsɛm pre   vo le ˈra
a   te   sempre   volerà,
to   you   always   will fly

e   fin   ˈlul ti mo   so ˈspir
e   fin   l'ultimo   sospir,
and   even   the last   sigh

ˈka ro   ˈno me   ˈtu o   sa ˈra
caro   nome,   tuo   sarà.
dear   name   yours   will be

il   ˈmi o   de ˈzir   a   te
Il   mio   desir   a   te
the   my   desire   to   you

oɲː ˈɲo ra   vo le ˈra
ognora   volerà!
always   will fly

TURANDOT

music: Giacomo Puccini
libretto: Giuseppe Adami and Renato Simoni (after an adaptation by Schiller of Count Carlo Gozzi's play *Turandotte,* also perhaps after *The Arabian Nights*)

Signore, ascolta!

siɲ: 'no re   a 'skol ta
Signore,   ascolta!
master   listen

a   siɲ: 'no re   a 'skol ta
Ah,   signore,   ascolta!
ah   master   listen

lju   non   'rɛd: dʒe   pju
Liù   non   regge   più!
Liù   not   withstands   more

si 'spɛt: tsa   il   kwɔr
Si spezza   il   cuor!
breaks   the   heart

a i 'mɛ   'kwan to   kam: 'mi no
Ahimè,   quanto   cammino
alas   how much   journey

kol   'tu o   'no me   nel: 'la ni ma
col   tuo   nome   nell'anima,
with the   your   name   in the soul

kol   'no me   'tu o   'sul: le   'lab: bra
col   nome   tuo   sulle   labbra!
with the   name   yours   upon the   lips

ma   se   il   'tu o   de 'sti no
Ma   se   il   tuo   destino,
but   if   the   your   destiny

do 'man   sa 'ra   de 'tʃi zo
doman,   sarà   deciso,
tomorrow   will be   decided

'no i   mor: 'rɛm   'sul: la   'stra da   del: le 'zi ljo
noi   morrem   sulla   strada   dell'esilio!
we   [we] will die   on the   path   of the exile

'e i   per de 'ra   'su o   'fiʎ: ʎo
Ei   perderà   suo   figlio...
he   will lose   his   son

'i o   'lom bra   dun   sor: 'ri zo
io   l'ombra   d'un   sorriso!
I   the trace   of a   smile

lju   non   'rɛd: dʒe   pju
Liù   non   regge   più!
Liù   not   withstands   more

a   pje 'ta
Ah,   pietà!
ah   [have] pity

Copyright © 1926 by G. Ricordi & Co.

Tu che di gel sei cinta

tu	ke	di	dʒɛl	'sɛ i	'tʃin ta
Tu	**che**	**di**	**gel**	**sei**	**cinta,**
you	*who*	*with*	*ice*	*are*	*girded*

da	'tan ta	'fjam: ma	'vin ta
da	**tanta**	**fiamma**	**vinta,**
by	*so much*	*passion*	*conquered*

la me 'ra i	'aŋ ke	tu
l'amerai	**anche**	**tu!**
him you will love	*also*	*you*

'pri ma di	'kwe sta	a u 'rɔ ra
Prima di	**questa**	**aurora,**
before	*this*	*dawn*

'i o	'kju do	'staŋ ka	ʎi	'ɔk: ki
io	**chiudo**	**stanca**	**gli**	**occhi,**
I	*[I] close*	*tired*	*the*	*eyes*

per 'ke	'eʎ: ʎi	'viŋ ka	aŋ 'ko ra
perchè	**egli**	**vinca**	**ancora...**
so that	*he*	*may conquer*	*again*

'e i	'viŋ ka	aŋ 'ko ra
ei	**vinca**	**ancora...**
he	*may conquer*	*again*

per	non	ve 'der lo	pju
per	**non**	**vederlo**	**più!**
for	*not*	*to see him*	*more*

Copyright © 1926 by G. Ricordi & Co.

ABOUT THE FRENCH IPA TRANSLITERATIONS
by Martha Gerhart

Following is a table of pronunciation for French lyric diction in singing as transliterated in this volume.

THE VOWELS

symbol	nearest equivalent in English	descriptive notes
[ɑ]	as in "f<u>a</u>ther"	the "dark 'a'"
[a]	in English only in dialect; comparable to the Italian "a"	the "bright 'a'"
[e]	no equivalent in English; as in the German "Schnee"	the "closed 'e'": [i] in the [ɛ] position
[ɛ]	as in "b<u>e</u>t"	the "open 'e'"
[i]	as in "f<u>ee</u>t"	
[o]	no equivalent in English as a pure vowel; approximately as in "<u>o</u>pen"	the "closed 'o'"
[ɔ]	as in "<u>ou</u>ght"	the "open 'o'"
[u]	as in "bl<u>ue</u>"	
[y]	no equivalent in English	[i] sustained with the lips rounded to a [u] position
[ø]	no equivalent in English	[e] sustained with the lips rounded almost to [u]
[œ] *	as in "<u>ea</u>rth" without pronouncing any "r"	[ɛ] with lips in the [ɔ] position
[ɑ̃]	no equivalent in English	the nasal "a": [ɔ] with nasal resonance added
[ɔ̃]	no equivalent in English	the nasal "o": [o] with nasal resonance added
[ɛ̃]	no equivalent in English	the nasal "e": as in English "c<u>a</u>t" with nasal resonance added
[œ̃]	no equivalent in English	the nasal "œ": as in English "<u>u</u>h, h<u>u</u>h" with nasal resonance added

* Some diction manuals transliterate the neutral, unstressed syllables in French as a "schwa" [ə].
Refer to authoritative published sources concerning such sophistications of French lyric diction.

THE SEMI-CONSONANTS

[ɥ]	no equivalent in English	a [y] in the tongue position of [i] and the lip position of [u]
[j]	as in "<u>e</u>we," "<u>y</u>es"	a "glide"
[w]	as in "<u>w</u>e," "<u>w</u>ant"	

THE CONSONANTS

[b]	as in "bad"	with a few exceptions
[c]	[k], as in "cart"	with some exceptions
[ç]	as in "sun"	when initial or medial, before *a*, *o*, or *u*
[d]	usually, as in "door"	becomes [t] in liaison
[f]	usually, as in "foot"	becomes [v] in liaison
[g]	usually, as in "gate"	becomes [k] in liaison; see also [ʒ]
[k]	as in "kite"	
[l]	as in "lift"	with some exceptions
[m]	as in "mint"	with a few exceptions
[n]	as in "nose"	with a few exceptions
[ɲ]	as in "onion"	almost always the pronunciation of the "gn" combination
[p]	as in "pass"	except when silent (final) and in a few rare words
[r] *	no equivalent in English	flipped (or occasionally rolled) "r"
[s]	as in "solo"	with exceptions; becomes [z] in liaison
[t]	as in "tooth"	with some exceptions
[v]	as in "voice"	
[x]	[ks] as in "extra," [gz] as in "exist," [z] as in "Oz," or [s] as in "sent"	becomes [z] in liaison
[z]	as in "zone"	with some exceptions
[ʒ]	as in "rouge"	usually, "g" when initial or mediant before *e*, *i*, or *y*; also, "j" in any position
[ʃ]	as in "shoe"	

* The conversational "uvular 'r'" is used in popular French song and cabaret but is not considered appropriate for singing in the classical repertoire.

LIAISON AND ELISION

Liaison is common in French. It is the sounding (linking) of a normally silent final consonant with the vowel (or mute h) beginning the next word. Its use follows certain rules; apart from the rules, the final choice as to whether or not to make a liaison depends on good taste and/or the advice of experts.

Examples of liaison, with their IPA:

      les oiseaux   est ici
      lɛ‿zwa zo   ɛ‿ti si

Elision is the linking of a consonant followed by a final unstressed *e* with the vowel (or mute *h*) beginning the next word.

    examples, with their IPA: elle est   votre âme
                                 ɛ‿lɛ   vɔ‿trɑ mœ

The linking symbol [‿] is given in these transliterations for both **elision** and for (recommended) **liaisons**.

CARMEN

music: Georges Bizet
libretto: Henri Meilhac and Ludovic Halévy (after the novel by Prosper Mérimée)

Je dis que rien ne m'épouvante

sɛ	dɛ	kɔ̃ trœ bɑ̃ dje	lœ	rœ fy	ɔr di nɛ rœ
C'est	**des**	**contrebandiers**	**le**	**refuge**	**ordinaire.**
this is	*of the*	*smugglers*	*the*	*refuge*	*usual*

il ɛ ti si ʒœ lœ vɛ re
Il est ici; je le verrai!
he is here I him shall see

e lœ dœ vwar kœ mɛ̃ po za sa mɛ rœ
Et le devoir que m'imposa sa mère—
and the duty which to me assigned his mother

sɑ̃ trɑ̃ ble ʒœ la kɔ̃ pli re
sans trembler je l'accomplirai.
without to tremble I it [I] shall accomplish

ʒœ di kœ rjɛ̃ nœ me pu vɑ̃ tœ
Je dis que rien ne m'épouvante.
I say that anything not me frightens

ʒœ di he las kœ ʒœ re pɔ̃ dœ mwa
Je dis, hélas! que je réponds de moi;
I say alas that I answer for myself

mɛ ʒe bo fɛ rœ la va jɑ̃ tœ
mais j'ai beau faire la vaillante...
but I pretend [to be] in vain the brave one

o fɔ̃ dy kœr ʒœ mœr de frwa
au fond du cœur je meurs d'effroi!
at the bottom of the heart I die of fright

sœ lɑ̃ sœ ljø so va ʒə
Seule en ce lieu sauvage—
alone in this place wild

tu tœ sœ lœ ʒe pœr
toute seule j'ai peur,
all alone I have fear

mɛ ʒe tɔr da vwar pœr
mais j'ai tort d'avoir peur.
but I am wrong of to have fear

vu mœ dɔ nœ re dy ku ra ʒə
Vous me donnerez du courage;
you to me will give of the courage

vu mœ pro tɛ ʒœ re sɛ ɲœr
vous me protégerez, Seigneur!
you me will protect Lord

ʒœ vɛ vwar de prɛ sɛ tœ fa mə
Je vais voir de près cette femme
I am going to see close to that woman

dɔ̃	lɛ‿	zar ti fi sœ	mo di	ɔ̃	fi ni
dont	**les**	**artifices**	**maudits**	**ont**	**fini**
of whom	*the*	*artifices*	*cursed*	*have*	*ended up*

par	fɛ‿	rœ̃	nɛ̃ fɑ mə
par	**faire**	**un**	**infâme**
by	*making*	*a*	*infamous person*

dœ	sœ lɥi	kœ	ʒɛ mɛ	ʒa dis
de	**celui**	**que**	**j'aimais**	**jadis!**
of	*the one*	*whom*	*I loved*	*of old*

ɛ‿	lɛ	dɑ̃ ʒø røz
Elle	**est**	**dangereuse...**
she	*is*	*dangerous*

ɛ‿	lɛ	bɛ lœ
elle	**est**	**belle!**
she	*is*	*beautiful*

mɛ	ʒœ	nœ	vø	pɑ‿	za vwar	pœr
Mais	**je**	**ne**	**veux**	**pas**	**avoir**	**peur!**
but	*I*	*not*	*want*	*[not]*	*to have*	*fear*

nɔ̃	nɔ̃	ʒœ	nœ	vø	pɑ‿	za vwar pœr
Non,	**non,**	**je**	**ne**	**veux**	**pas**	**avoir peur!**
no	*no*	*I*	*not*	*want*	*[not]*	*to have fear*

ʒœ	par lœ re	o	dœ vɑ̃‿	tɛ lə
Je	**parlerai**	**haut**	**devant**	**elle...**
I	*will speak*	*loudly*	*in front of*	*her*

a	sɛ ɲœr	vu	mœ	prɔ te ʒœ re
Ah!	**Seigneur,**	**vous**	**me**	**protégerez!**
ah	*Lord*	*you*	*me*	*will protect*

prɔ te ʒe mwa	o	sɛ ɲœr
Protégez-moi!	**Ô**	**Seigneur!**
protect me	*o*	*Lord*

dɔ ne mwa	dy	ku ra ʒœ
Donnez-moi	**du**	**courage!**
give me	*of the*	*courage*

prɔ te ʒe mwa	sɛ ɲœr
Protégez-moi,	**Seigneur!**
protect me	*Lord*

LES CONTES D'HOFFMANN

music: Jacques Offenbach
libretto: Jules Barbier and Michel Carré (after stories of E.T.A. Hoffmann)

Elle a fui, la tourterelle!

ɛ	la	fɥi	la	tur tœ rɛ lœ
Elle	**a**	**fui,**	**la**	**tourterelle!**
she	*has*	*fled*	*the*	*turtle dove*

a	su vœ nir	trɔ	du
Ah!	**souvenir**	**trop**	**doux!**
ah	*memory*	*too*	*sweet*

i ma ʒœ	trɔ	kry ɛ lœ
Image	**trop**	**cruelle!**
image	*too*	*cruel*

he lɑs	a	mɛ	ʒœ nu
Hélas!	**à**	**mes**	**genoux**
alas	*at*	*my*	*knees*

ʒœ	lã tã	ʒœ	lœ	vwa
je	**l'entends,**	**je**	**le**	**vois!**
I	*him hear*	*I*	*him*	*see*

ɛ	la	fɥi	la	tur tœ rɛ lœ
Elle	**a**	**fui,**	**la**	**tourterelle.**
she	*has*	*fled*	*the*	*turtle dove*

ɛ	la	fɥi	lwɛ̃	dœ	twa
Elle	**a**	**fui**	**loin**	**de**	**toi;**
she	*has*	*fled*	*far*	*from*	*you*

mɛ	zɛ	lɛ	tu ʒur	fi dɛ lœ
mais	**elle**	**est**	**toujours**	**fidèle**
but	*she*	*is*	*always*	*faithful*

e	tœ	gar dœ	sa	fwa
et	**te**	**garde**	**sa**	**foi.**
and	*for you*	*keeps*	*her*	*faith*

mɔ̃	bjɛ̃ nɛ me	ma	vwa	ta pɛ lœ
Mon	**bien-aimé,**	**ma**	**voix**	**t'appelle.**
my	*beloved*	*my*	*voice*	*you calls*

wi	tu	mɔ̃	kœ	rɛ	ta	twa
Oui,	**tout**	**mon**	**cœur**	**est**	**à**	**toi.**
yes	*all*	*my*	*heart*	*is*	*to*	*you*

ʃɛ rœ	flœr	ki	vjɛ̃ de klɔ rœ
Chère	**fleur**	**qui**	**viens d'éclore,**
dear	*flower*	*which*	*has just flowered*

par pi tje	re pɔ̃ mwa
par pitié,	**réponds-moi!**
for pity's sake	*answer me*

twa	ki	sɛ	sil	mɛ	mã kɔ rœ
toi	**qui**	**sais**	**s'il**	**m'aime**	**encore,**
you	*who*	*know*	*if he*	*me loves*	*still*

sil	mœ	gar de	sa	fwa
s'il	**me**	**garde**	**sa**	**foi!**
if he	*for me*	*keeps*	*his*	*faith*

mɔ̃	bjɛ̃ ne me	ma	vwa	tɛ̃ plɔ rœ
Mon	**bien-aimé,**	**ma**	**voix**	**t'implore.**
my	*beloved*	*my*	*voice*	*you implores*

a	kœ	tɔ̃	kœr	vjɛ	na mwa
Ah!	**que**	**ton**	**cœur**	**vienne**	**à moi.**
ah	*that*	*your*	*heart*	*may come*	*to me*

FAUST
music: Charles Gounod
libretto: Jules Barbier and Michel Carré (after the drama by Johann Wolfgang von Goethe)

Ah! Je ris de me voir
(The Jewel Song)

kœ	vwa ʒœ	la
Que	**vois-je**	**là?**
what	*see I*	*there*

du	sœ	ri ʃœ	kɔ frɛ	pø til	vœ nir
D'où	**ce**	**riche**	**coffret**	**peut-il**	**venir?**
from where	*that*	*splendid*	*small chest*	*can it*	*[to] come*

ʒœ	no	zi	tu ʃe	e	pur tɑ̃
Je	**n'ose**	**y**	**toucher,**	**et**	**pourtant...**
I	*not dare*	*it*	*[to] touch*	*and*	*yet*

vwa si	la	kle	ʒœ	krwa
Voici	**la**	**clef,**	**je**	**crois!**
here is	*the*	*key*	*I*	*believe*

si	ʒœ	lu vrɛ
Si	**je**	**l'ouvrais!**
if	*I*	*it should open*

ma	mɛ̃	trɑ̃ blœ	pur kwa
Ma	**main**	**tremble!**	**Pourquoi?**
my	*hand*	*trembles*	*why*

ʒœ	nœ	fɛ	ɑ̃	lu vrɑ̃
Je	**ne**	**fais,**	**en**	**l'ouvrant,**
I	*not*	*do*	*in*	*it opening*

rjɛ̃	dœ	mal	ʒœ	sy po zœ
rien	**de**	**mal,**	**je**	**suppose!**
anything	*of*	*bad*	*I*	*suppose*

o	djø	kœ	dœ	bi ʒu
Ô	**Dieu!**	**que**	**de**	**bijoux!**
Oh	*God*	*what*	*of*	*jewels*

ɛ	sœ	rɛ vœ	ʃar mɑ̃	ki	me blu i
Est-ce	**un**	**rêve**	**charmant**	**qui**	**m'éblouit,**
is this	*a*	*dream*	*charming*	*which*	*me dazzles*

u	si	ʒœ	vɛ jœ
ou	**si**	**je**	**veille?**
or	*if*	*I*	*am awake*

IPA	French	English
mɛ zjø nɔ̃ ʒa mɛ vy	**Mes yeux n'ont jamais vu**	my eyes not have ever seen

IPA	French	English
dœ ri ʃɛ sə pa rɛ jœ	**de richesse pareille!**	of opulence equal

IPA	French	English
si ʒɔ zɛ sœ lœ mã	**Si j'osais seulement**	if I dared only

IPA	French	English
mœ pa re œ̃ mɔ mã	**me parer un moment**	myself to adorn a moment

IPA	French	English
dœ sɛ pã dã dɔ rɛ jœ	**de ces pendants d'oreille!**	with these drop earrings

IPA	French	English
a vwa si ʒys tœ mã	**Ah! Voici justement,**	ah here is deservedly

IPA	French	English
o fɔ̃ dœ la ka sɛ tœ	**au fond de la cassette:**	at the bottom of the box

IPA	French	English
œ̃ mi rwar	**un miroir!**	a mirror

IPA	French	English
kɔ mã nɛ trœ pɑ kɔ kɛ tœ	**Comment n'être pas coquette?**	how not to be coquette

IPA	French	English
a ʒœ ri dœ mœ vwar	**Ah! Je ris de me voir**	ah I laugh of myself to see

IPA	French	English
si bɛ lã sœ mi rwar	**si belle en ce miroir!**	so beautiful in this mirror

IPA	French	English
ɛ sœ twa mar gœ ri tœ	**Est-ce toi, Marguerite?**	is this you Marguerite

IPA	French	English
re pɔ̃ mwa re pɔ̃ vi tœ	**Réponds-moi; réponds vite!**	answer me answer quickly

IPA	French	English
nɔ̃ sœ nɛ ply twa	**Non! ce n'est plus toi!**	no this not is more you

IPA	French	English
sœ nɛ ply tɔ̃ vi za ʒœ	**Ce n'est plus ton visage;**	this not is more your face

IPA	French	English
sɛ la fi jœ dœ̃ rwa	**c'est la fille d'un roi**	it is the daughter of a king

kɔ̃	sa ly	o	pɑ sa ʒœ
qu'on	**salue**	**au**	**passage!**
whom one	*bows to*	*at the*	*passing*

a	sil	e tɛ‿	ti si
Ah,	**s'il**	**était**	**ici!**
ah	*if he*	*was*	*here*

sil	mœ	vwaje‿	tɛ̃ si
S'il	**me**	**voyait**	**ainsi!**
if he	*me*	*saw*	*like this*

kɔ‿	my nœ	dœ mwa zɛ lœ
Comme	**une**	**demoiselle**
as	*a*	*young lady*

il	mœ	tru vœ rɛ	bɛ lœ
il	**me**	**trouverait**	**belle!**
he	*me*	*would find*	*beautiful*

a ʃœ vɔ̃	la	me ta mɔr fo zœ
Achevons	**la**	**métamorphose.**
let's complete	*the*	*transformation*

il mœ tar‿	dɑ̃ kɔr	de sɛ je
Il me tarde	**encor**	**d'essayer**
I am anxious	*still*	*of to try*

lœ	bra sœ lɛ	e	lœ kɔ lje
le	**bracelet**	**et**	**le collier!**
the	*bracelet*	*and*	*the necklace*

dø	sɛ	kɔ‿	my nœ	mɛ̃
Dieu!	**c'est**	**comme**	**une**	**main,**
God	*it is*	*like*	*a*	*hand*

ki	syr	mɔ̃	bra	sœ po zœ
qui	**sur**	**mon**	**bras**	**se pose!**
which	*on*	*my*	*arm*	*puts itself*

a
Ah!...
ah

MANON
music: Jules Massenet
libretto: Henri Meilhac and Philippe Gille (after the novel *L'Histoire du Chevalier des Grieux et de Manon Lescaut* by Abbé Prévost)

Adieu, notre petite table

a lɔ̃ il lœ fo
Allons! il le faut!
come on it is necessary

pur lɥi mɛ mœ
pour lui même!
for him himself

mɔ̃ po vrœ ʃœ va lje
Mon pauvre chevalier!
my poor chevalier

o wi sɛ lɥi kœ ʒɛ mœ
Oh! oui, c'est lui que j'aime!
oh yes it is he whom I love

e pur tɑ̃ ʒe zi to ʒur dɥi
Et pourtant, j'hésite aujourd'hui!
and yet I hesitate today

nɔ̃ ʒœ nœ sɥi ply di ɲœ dœ lɥi
Non, je ne suis plus digne de lui!
no I not am longer worthy of him

ʒɑ̃ tɑ̃ sɛ tœ vwa ki mɑ̃ trɛ nœ
J'entends cette voix qui m'entraîne
I hear that voice which me seduces

kɔ̃ trœ ma vɔ lɔ̃ te
contre ma volonté:
against my will

ma nɔ̃ ma nɔ̃ ty sœ ra rɛ nœ
«Manon! Manon, tu seras reine—
Manon Manon you will be queen

rɛ nœ par la bo te
reine par la beauté!»
queen through the beauty

ʒœ nœ sɥi kœ fɛ blɛ sœ
Je ne suis que faiblesse
I not am [anything] but weakness

e kœ fra ʒi li te
et que fragilité!
and but frailty

a mal gre mwa
Ah! malgré moi
ah despite myself

ʒœ sɑ̃ ku le mɛ lar mœ
je sens couler mes larmes
I feel to flow my tears

dœ vɑ̃ sɛ rɛ vœ ze fa se
devant ces rêves effacés!
in the face of those dreams obliterated

la vœ nir	o ra til	lɛ	ʃar mœ	
L'avenir	**aura-t-il**	**les**	**charmes**	
the future	*will it have*	*the*	*charms*	

dœ	sɛ	bo	ʒur	de ʒa	pɑ se
de	**ces**	**beaux**	**jours**	**déjà**	**passés?**
of	*those*	*beautiful*	*days*	*already*	*passed*

a djø	nɔ trœ	pœ ti tœ	ta blœ
Adieu,	**notre**	**petite**	**table,**
farewell	*our*	*little*	*table*

ki	nu	re y ni	si	su vɑ̃
qui	**nous**	**réunit**	**si**	**souvent!**
which	*us*	*re-united*	*so*	*often*

a djø	nɔ trœ	pœ ti tœ	ta blœ
Adieu,	**notre**	**petite**	**table,**
farewell	*our*	*little*	*table*

si	grɑ̃ dœ	pur	nu	sœ pɑ̃ dɑ̃
si	**grande**	**pour**	**nous**	**cependant!**
so	*big*	*for*	*us*	*however*

ɔ̃	tjɛ̃	sɛ	ti ni ma ʒi na blœ
On	**tient,**	**c'est**	**inimaginable,**
one	*takes up*	*it is*	*unbelievable*

si	pø	dœ	pla sœ	ɑ̃	sœ sɛ rɑ̃
si	**peu**	**de**	**place**	**en**	**se serrant!**
so	*little*	*of*	*space*	*in*	*sitting close together*

a djø	nɔ trœ	pœ ti tœ	ta blœ
Adieu,	**notre**	**petite**	**table!**
farewell	*our*	*little*	*table*

œ̃	mɛ mœ	vɛ	re tɛ	lœ	no trœ
Un	**même**	**verre**	**était**	**le**	**nôtre;**
a	*same*	*glass*	*was*	*the*	*ours*

ʃa kœ̃	dœ	nu	kɑ̃	til	by vɛ
chacun	**de**	**nous**	**quand**	**il**	**buvait**
each	*of*	*us*	*when*	*he*	*was drinking*

i	ʃɛr ʃɛ	lɛ	lɛ vrœ	dœ	lo trœ
y	**cherchait**	**les**	**lèvres**	**de**	**l'autre.**
there	*sought*	*the*	*lips*	*of*	*the other*

a	poː	vra mi	kɔ̃	mil	mɛ mɛ
Ah!	**pauvre**	**ami,**	**comme**	**il**	**m'aimait!**
ah	*poor*	*friend*	*how*	*he*	*me loved*

a djø	nɔ trœ	pœ ti tœ	ta blœ
Adieu,	**notre**	**petite**	**table!**
farewell	*our*	*little*	*table*

ROMÉO ET JULIETTE
music: Charles Gounod
libretto: Jules Barbier and Michel Carré (after the tragedy by William Shakespeare)

Ah! Je veux vivre
(Juliette's Waltz Song)

a	ʒœ	vø	vi vrœ	dã	lœ	rɛ vœ
Ah!	**Je**	**veux**	**vivre**	**dans**	**le**	**rêve**
ah	*I*	*want*	*to live*	*in*	*the*	*dream*

ki	mã‿ni vrœ	sœ	ʒu‿	rã kɔr
qui	**m'enivre**	**ce**	**jour**	**encor!**
which	*me inebriates*	*this*	*day*	*still*

du sœ	flɑ mœ	ʒœ	tœ	gar de
Douce	**flamme,**	**je**	**te**	**garde**
sweet	*flame*	*I*	*you*	*keep*

dã	mɔ̃‿	na mœ	kɔ‿	mœ	tre zɔr
dans	**mon**	**âme**	**comme**	**un**	**trésor!**
in	*my*	*soul*	*like*	*a*	*treasure*

sɛ‿	ti vrɛ sœ	dœ	ʒœ nɛ sœ
Cette	**ivresse**	**de**	**jeunesse**
this	*intoxication*	*of*	*youth*

nœ	dyr	e lɑs	kœ̃	ʒur
ne	**dure,**	**hélas!**	**qu'un**	**jour.**
not	*lasts*	*alas*	*but a*	*day*

pɥi	vjɛ̃	lœ rœ	u	lɔ̃	plœ rœ
Puis	**vient**	**l'heure**	**où**	**l'on**	**pleure;**
then	*comes*	*the hour*	*when*	*the one*	*weeps*

lœ	kœr	sɛ‿	da	la mur
le	**cœur**	**cède**	**à**	**l'amour,**
the	*heart*	*yields*	*to*	*the love*

e	lœ	bɔ‿nœr	fɥi	sã	rœ tur
et	**le**	**bonheur**	**fuit**	**sans**	**retour!**
and	*the*	*happiness*	*flies away*	*without*	*return*

a	ʒœ	vø	vi vrœ	dã	lœ	rɛ vœ
Ah!	**Je**	**veux**	**vivre**	**dans**	**le**	**rêve**
ah	*I*	*want*	*to live*	*in*	*the*	*dream*

ki	mã‿ni vrœ	lɔ̃ tã‿	zã kɔr
qui	**m'enivre**	**longtemps**	**encor!**
which	*me inebriates*	*long time*	*still*

lwɛ̃	dœ	li vɛr	mɔ ro zœ
Loin	**de**	**l'hiver**	**morose**
far	*from*	*the winter*	*gloomy*

lɛ sœ mwa	sɔ mɛ je
laisse-moi	**sommeiller**
let me	*[to] slumber*

e	rɛ spi re	la	ro‿ zœ
et	**respirer**	**la**	**rose**
and	*[to] breathe*	*the*	*rose*

za vɑ̃	dœ		lə fœ je
avant	**de**		**l'effeuiller.**
before	*of*		*it to shed its petals*

a	du sœ	flɑ mœ
Ah!	**Douce**	**flamme,**
ah	*sweet*	*flame*

rɛ stœ	dɑ	mɔ̃	nɑ mœ
reste	**dans**	**mon**	**âme**
remain	*in*	*my*	*soul*

kɔ̃	mœ̃	du	tre zɔr
comme	**un**	**doux**	**trésor**
as	*a*	*sweet*	*treasure*

lɔ̃ tɑ̃	zɑ̃ kɔr
longtemps	**encor!**
long time	*still*

Note: at the very end, with a breath:

lɔ̃ tɑ̃	ɑ̃ kɔr
longtemps	**encor!**

ABOUT THE GERMAN IPA TRANSLITERATIONS
by Irene Spiegelman

TRANSLATIONS

As every singer has experienced, word-by-word translations are usually awkward, often not understandable, especially in German where the verb usually is split up with one part in second position of the main clause and the rest at the end of the sentence. Sometimes it is a second verb, sometimes it is a little word that looks like a preposition. Since prepositions never come by themselves, these are usually *separable prefixes to the verb*. In order to look up the meaning of the verb this prefix has to be reunited with the verb in order to find the correct meaning in the dictionary. They cannot be looked up by themselves. Therefore, in the word-by-word translation they are marked with [1]) and do not show any words.

Note: In verbs with separable prefixes, the prefix gets the emphasis. If a separable prefix appears at the end of the sentence, it still needs to be stressed and since many of them start with vowels they even might be glottaled for emphasis.

Also, there are many *reflexive verbs* in German that are not reflexive in English, also the reflexive version of a verb in German often means something very different than the meaning found if the verb is looked up by itself. Reflexive pronouns that are grammatically necessary but do not have a meaning by themselves do not show a translation underneath. They are marked with [2]).

Another difference in the use of English and German is that German is using the Present Perfect Tense of the verb where English prefers the use of the Simple Past of the verb. In cases like that, the translation appears under the conjugated part of the verb and none underneath the past participle of the verb at the end of the sentence. Those cases are marked with [3]).

One last note concerning the translations: English uses possessive pronouns much more often then German does. So der/die/das in German have at appropriate points been translated as my/your/his.

PRONUNCIATION (EXTENDED IPA SYMBOLS)

The IPA symbols that have been used for the German arias are basically those used in Langenscheidt dictionaries. Other publications have refined some symbols, but after working with young singers for a long time, I find that they usually don't remember which is which sign when the ones for long closed vowels (a and ɑ, or ʏ and y) are too close, and especially with the signs for the open and closed u-umlauts they usually cannot tell which they handwrote into their scores. To make sure that a vowel should be closed there is ":" behind the symbol, i.e. [byːp laɪn]

After having been encouraged to sing on a vowel as long as possible, often the consonants are cut too short. The rule is, "**Vowels can be used to make your voice shine, consonants will help your interpretation!**" This is very often totally neglected in favor of long vowels, even when the vowels are supposed to be short. Therefore, double consonants show up here in the IPA line. This suggests that they should at least not be neglected. There are voiced consonants on which it is easy to sing (l, m, n) and often give the text an additional dimension. That is not true for explosive consonants (d, t, k), but they open the vowels right in front of them. So the double consonants in these words serve here as reminders. German does not require to double the consonants the way Italian does, but that Italian technique might help to move more quickly to the consonant, and therefore open the vowel or at least don't stretch it, which sometimes turns it into a word with a different meaning altogether.

One idea that is heard over and over again is: "There is no legato in German." The suggestions that are marked here with ⇨ in the IPA line show that **that is not true.** Always elided can be words ending in a vowel with the next word beginning with a vowel. Words that end with a -t sound can be combined with the next word that starts with a t- or a d-. A word ending in -n can be connected to the following beginning -n. But words ending in consonants can also be elided with the next word starting with a vowel. (example: Dann [dan⇨n] könnt' [kœn⇨n⇨] ich [⇨tɪç] mit [mɪt] Fürsten ['fyr stən] mich ['mɛs⇨sən]). In this example, the arrow symbol suggests to use the double consonant, but also that the end-t in "könnt'" could be used at the beginning of "ich" which makes the word "ich" much less important (which it usually is in German), and could help to shape the words "Fürsten" and "messen" with more importance.

Within the IPA line, sometimes the "⇨" symbol is only at the end of a word and means that combining this word with the next is absolutely possible if it helps the interpretation of the text or the singer does not want to interrupt the beauty of the musical line. The same fact is true if the "⇨" symbol appears within a word and suggests combining syllables. (Since English syllables are viewed differently than German syllables, the IPA line is broken down into German syllables with suggestions for vocal combinations.) The only consonant that should not be combined with the next word is "r," because there are too many combinations that form new words (example: der Eine, the one and only, should not become [deː raɪ nə], the pure one).

One last remark about pronunciation that seems to have become an issue in the last few years: How does one pronounce the a-umlaut = ä. Some singers have been told in their diction classes that ä is pronounced like a closed e. That may be the case in casual language and can be heard on German television. But when the texts that we are dealing with were written the sound was either a long or short open e sound ['mɛː tçən, ʃpɛːt, 'hɛl tə].

Considering the language, how does one make one's voice shine and still use the text for a sensible interpretation? Look for the words within a phrase that are important to you as the interpreter, as the person who believes what he/she is conveying. In those words use the consonants as extensively as possible. [zzzeː lə] and [llliː bə] are usually more expressive than [zeː lə] and [liː bə] , also glottal the beginning vowels. Use the surrounding words for singing legato and show off the voice.

The IPA line not only shows correct pronunciation but is also giving guidelines for interpretation. For instance, R's may be rolled or flipped, or words may be connected or separated at any time as long as they help you with your feeling for the drama of the text. But you are the person who has to decide! Be discriminating! Know what you want to say! Your language will fit with the music perfectly.

THE "R" IN GERMAN DICTION

When most Germans speak an "r" in front of a vowel, it is a sound produced between the far back of the tongue and the uvula, almost like a gargling sound. The r's at the end of syllables take on different sounds and often have a vowel-like quality.

In classical singing, the practice is to use "Italian r's". Since trilling the r at the tip of the tongue seems to be easy for most singers, many texts are rendered with any overdone r's, which are remotely possible. As a result, the r's take over the whole text and diminish the meaning and phrasing of the sentences. By being discriminating in using rolled r's in an opera text, the phrasing, i.e. interpretation, as well as the chance of understanding the sung text can be improved.

Essentially, there are three categories of words with different suggestions about the use of r's:

ALWAYS ROLL THE R	END-R'S IN SHORT ONE-SYLLABLE WORDS	END-R'S IN PREFIXES AND SUFFIXES
a) before vowels: Rose ['roː zə] tragen ['traː gən] sprechen ['ʃprɛː xən] Trug [truːk] führen ['fyː rən] b) after vowels in the main syllable of the word: bergen ['bɛr gən] Herz [hɛrts] Schwert [ʃveːrt] durch [dʊrç] geworben [gə 'vɔr bən] hart [hart]	End-r's in short one-syllable words that have a closed vowel can be replaced with a short a-vowel, marked in the IPA line with ᵃ. der [deː ᵃ] er [eː ᵃ] wir [viː ᵃ] hier [hiː ᵃ] vor [foː ᵃ] nur [nuː ᵃ] **Note:** **After an a-vowel a replacement of r by ᵃ would not sound. Therefore end-r's after any a should be rolled.** **war [vaːr]** **gar [gaːr]**	Prefixes: ver- er- zer- Here, e and r could be pronounced as a schwa-sound, almost like a short open e combined with a very short ᵃ. If desired, the r could also be flipped with one little flip in order not to overpower the main part of the word which is coming up. In the IPA-line this is marked with ʀ. verbergen [fɛʀ 'bɛr gən] erklären [ɛʀ 'klɛː rən] Suffix: -er These suffixes are most of the time not important for the interpretation of the text. Therefore, the schwa-sound as explained above works in most cases very well. It is marked in the IPA-line with ɚ. e-Suffixes are marked with ə. guter ['guː tɚ] gute ['guː tə] Winter ['vɪn tɚ] Meistersinger ['maɪ stɚ sɪ ŋɚ] (compound noun, both parts end in -er)

FIDELIO

music: Ludwig van Beethoven
libretto: Josef Sonnleithner; revised by Stephan von Breuning and Georg Friedrich Treitschke (after Jean Nicolas Bouilly's play *Léonore, ou L'Amour Conjugal*)

O wär' ich schon mit dir vereint

oː vɛːr ɪç ʃoːn mɪt⇨ diːᵃ fɛʀ ˈaɪnt	O wär' ich schon mit dir vereint,	Oh, were I already with you united
ʊnt⇨ dyr⇨ ftə man dɪç ˈnɛn⇨ nən	und dürfte Mann dich nennen!	and were allowed husband you to call!
aɪn mɛː⇨ tçən darf jaː vas⇨ ɛs maɪnt	Ein Mädchen darf ja, was es meint,	A young girl may after all what she thinks
tsuːᵃ ˈhɛlf tə nuːᵃ bə kɛn⇨ nən	zur Hälfte nur bekennen!	just half only admit!
dɔx vɛnn⇨ ɪç nɪçt ɛʀ ˈʀøː tən mʊss	Doch wenn ich nicht erröten muss	But, when I not blush must
ɔp ˈaɪ nəm ˈvar mən ˈhɛr tsəns kʊs	ob einem warmen Herzenskuss,	because of a warm heartfelt kiss
vɛnn⇨ nɪçts ʊns⇨ ʃtøːrt aʊf ˈeːr dən	wenn nichts uns stört auf Erden...	when nothing us will disturb on earth...
diː ˈhɔff nʊŋ ʃoːn ɛʀ ˈfʏllt⇨ diː brʊst	Die Hoffnung schon erfüllt die Brust	(The) hope already is filling my heart
mɪt ˈʊn aʊs ˈʃpɛç lɪç ˈzyː sɐ lʊst	mit unausssprechlich süßer Lust;	with indescribable sweet desire;
viː glʏk⇨ lɪç vɪll⇨ ɪç ˈveːr dən	wie glücklich will ich werden!	how happy will I be!
ɪn ˈruː (h)ə ʃtɪl⇨ lɐ ˈhɔys lɪç kaɪt	In Ruhe stiller Häuslichkeit	In (the) quiet of peaceful domesticity
ɛʀ ˈvax⇨ ɪç ˈjeː dən ˈmɔr gən	erwach' ich jeden Morgen.	awake I every morning.
viːᵃ ˈgryː sən ʊns mɪt⇨ ˈtsɛːr⇨ tlɪç kaɪt	Wir grüßen uns mit Zärtlichkeit;	We will greet each other with tenderness,

deːᵃ	flaɪs	fɛʀ ˈʃɔyçt⇒	diː	ˈzɔr gən
der	**Fleiß**	**verscheucht**	**die**	**Sorgen.**
(the)	*hard work*	*drives away*	*(the)*	*anxieties.*

ʊnt	ɪst	diː	ˈar ˈbaɪt	ˈap gə ˈtan
Und	**ist**	**die**	**Arbeit**	**abgetan,**
And	*is*	*(the)*	*work*	*is finished*

dann	ʃlaɪçt	diː	ˈhɔl də	naxt	hɛ ˈran
dann	**schleicht**	**die**	**holde**	**Nacht**	**heran;**
then	*descends*	*the*	*lovely*	*night*	¹⁾

dann	ruːn	viːᵃ	fɔn	bə ˈʃveːr dən
dann	**ruh'n**	**wir**	**von**	**Beschwerden.**
then	*will rest*	*we*	*from*	*sorrows.*

viː	vɪll⇒	ɪç	ˈglʏk⇒ lɪç	ˈveːr dən
Wie	**will**	**ich**	**glücklich**	**werden!**
How	*want*	*I*	*happy*	*to be!*

¹⁾ Prefix to the verb „heranschleichen" (descend)

DER FREISCHÜTZ
music: Carl Maria von Weber
libretto: Johann Friedrich Kind (after a story by Johann August Apel and Friedrich Laun and Gothic legend)

Kommt ein schlanker Bursch gegangen

kɔmmt⇒	aɪn	ˈʃlaŋ kɐ	bʊrʃ	ge ˈga ŋən
Kommt	**ein**	**schlanker**	**Bursch**	**gegangen,**
Should	*a*	*slender*	*fellow*	*come along,*

blɔnt	fɔn	ˈlɔk⇒ kən	ˈoː dɐ	braʊn
blond	**von**	**Locken**	**oder**	**braun,**
blond	*(of)*	*hair*	*or*	*brunette,*

hɛl⇒l	fɔn	aʊk⇒	ʊnt	roːt	fɔn	ˈva ŋən
hell	**von**	**Aug'**	**und**	**rot**	**von**	**Wangen,**
bright	*(of)*	*eyes*	*and*	*rosy*	*(of)*	*cheeks,*

aɪ	nax	deːm	kan⇒n	man	voːl	ʃaʊn
ei,	**nach**	**dem**	**kann**	**man**	**wohl**	**schau'n!**
well,	*for*	*that one*	*can*	*one*	*certainly*	*look out!*

tsvar	ʃlɛːkt	man	das	aʊk	aʊfs	ˈmiː dɐ
Zwar	**schlägt**	**man**	**das**	**Aug'**	**aufs**	**Mieder**
Of course	*lowers*	*one*	*the*	*eyes*	*to the*	*bodice*

nax	fɛʀ ˈʃɛːm tɐ	mɛː⇒ tçən	aːrt
nach	**verschämter**	**Mädchen**	**Art;**
according to	*bashful*	*young girls*	*manner,*

dɔx	fɛʀ ˈʃtoː lən	heːpt	mans	ˈviː dɐ
doch	**verstohlen**	**hebt**	**man's**	**wieder,**
but	*furtively*	*raises*	*one them*	*again,*

vɛnns	das	ˈhɛrr çən	nɪçt	gə ˈvaːrt
wenn's	**das**	**Herrchen**	**nicht**	**gewahrt.**
wenn it's	*by the*	*young man*	*not being*	*noticed.*

IPA	German	English
'zɔll tən ja zɪç 'blɪk⇨ kə 'fɪn dən	**Sollten ja sich Blicke finden,**	*Should perhaps each other glances find,*
nu:n vas hat⇨ das aʊx fy:ᵃ no:t	**nun, was hat das auch für Not?**	*now, what harbors that possibly kind of danger?*
man vɪrt⇨ drʊm nɪçt glaɪç ɛʀ 'blɪn dən	**Man wird drum nicht gleich erblinden,**	*One will from that not right away be blinded,*
wɪrt⇨ man aʊx⇨ aɪn 've: nɪç ro:t	**wird man auch ein wenig rot.**	*becomes one even a little flushed.*
blɪk⇨ kçən hɪn ʊnt blɪk⇨ k hɛ 'ry: bɚ	**Blickchen hin und Blick herüber,**	*Little glance over and glance back,*
bɪs de:ᵃ mʊn⇨ ⇨tsɪç aʊx vas traʊt	**bis der Mund sich auch was traut.**	*until the mouth ²⁾ also something dares.*
e:ᵃ zɔyftst 'ʃø:n stə	**Er seufzt: Schönste!**	*He sighs: most beautiful one*
zi: ʃprɪçt 'li: bɚ	**Sie spricht: Lieber!**	*She says: Dearest;*
balt haɪsts 'brɔy ti: gam ʊnt braʊt	**Bald heißt's Bräutigam und Braut.**	*Soon they are groom and bride.*
'ɪm⇨ mɚ 'nɛ: ɚ 'li: bə 'lɔy⇨ tçən	**Immer näher, liebe Leutchen,**	*Closer and closer, dear folks,*
vɔl⇨lt i:ᵃ mɪç ɪm 'kran tsə ze:n	**wollt ihr mich im Kranze seh'n?**	*want you me in the bridal wreath see?*
gɛlt das⇨ ɪst aɪn 'nɛt⇨ təs 'brɔy⇨ tçən	**Gelt! das ist ein nettes Bräutchen,**	*Isn't it true, that is a pretty little bride,*
ʊnt⇨ de:ᵃ bʊrʃ nɪçt 'mɪn dɚ ʃø:n	**und der Bursch nicht minder schön!**	*and the fellow not less attractive!*

²⁾ Reflexive pronoun for a verb that is not reflexive in English (sich trauen = dare)

DER SCHAUSPIELDIREKTOR
music: Wolfgang Amadeus Mozart
libretto: Gottlieb Stephanie, the younger

Bester Jüngling

IPA	German	English
'bɛ stɐ	**Bester**	*Dear*
'jʏŋ lɪŋ	**Jüngling,**	*young man,*
mɪt	**mit**	*with*
ɛnt⇨ 'tsʏk⇨ kən	**Entzücken**	*enchantment*

neː⇨	mɪç	'daɪ nə	'liː bə	an
nehm'	**ich**	**deine**	**Liebe**	**an,**
accept	*I*	*your*	*love.*	[1]

daː	ɪn	'daɪ nən	'hɔl dən	'blɪk⇨ kən
da	**in**	**deinen**	**holden**	**Blicken**
for	*in*	*your*	*sweet*	*glances*

ɪç	maɪn	glʏkk	ɛnt⇨ 'dɛk⇨ kən	kann
ich	**mein**	**Glück**	**entdecken**	**kann.**
I	*my*	*happiness*	*discover*	*can.*

aː bɐ	ax	vɛn	'dyː strəs	'lai dən
Aber	**ach,**	**wenn**	**düst'res**	**Leiden**
But	*ah,*	*if*	*sad*	*suffering*

'ʊn zrɐ	'liː bə	'fɔl gən	zɔll
unsrer	**Liebe**	**folgen**	**soll,**
our	*love*	*endure*	*is to,*

'loː nən	diːs	deːɐ	'liː bə	'frɔy dən
lohnen	**dies**	**der**	**Liebe**	**Freuden?**
is worth	*this*	*the*	*love's*	*joys?*

'jʏŋ lɪŋ	das	bə 'dɛŋ kə	voːl
Jüngling,	**das**	**bedenke**	**wohl!**
Young man,	*that*	*consider*	*carefully!*

nɪç⇨	tsɪst	miːɐ	zoː	veːrt⇨	ʊnt⇨	'tɔy ɐ
Nichts	**ist**	**mir**	**so**	**wert**	**und**	**teuer,**
Nothing	*is*	*to me*	*as*	*worthy*	*and*	*precious*

als	daɪn	hɛrts⇨	ʊnt⇨	'daɪ nə	hant
als	**dein**	**Herz**	**und**	**deine**	**Hand.**
as	*your*	*heart*	*and*	*your*	*hand.*

fɔll	fɔm	'raɪn stən	'liː bəs 'fɔy ɐ
Voll	**vom**	**reinsten**	**Liebesfeuer**
Full	*of the*	*purest*	*ardor of love*

geː⇨	⇨pɪç	diːɐ	maɪn	hɛrts	tsʊm	pfant
geb'	**ich**	**dir**	**mein**	**Herz**	**zum**	**Pfand.**
give	*I*	*to you*	*my*	*heart*	*in*	*pledge.*

[1] Prefix to the verb "annehmen" (accept)

DIE ZAUBERFLÖTE
music: Wolfgang Amadeus Mozart
libretto: Emanuel Schikaneder (loosely based on a fairy tale by Wieland)

Ach, ich fühl's

ax⇨	Iç	ˈfyːls	ɛs⇨	Ist⇨	fɛᵃ ˈʃvʊn dən
Ach,	**ich**	**fühl's,**	**es**	**ist**	**verschwunden,**
Ah,	*I*	*feel it,*	*it*	*has*	*vanished,*

ˈeː viç	hɪn	deːᵃ	ˈliː bə	ˈglʏk
ewig	**hin**	**der**	**Liebe**	**Glück!**
forever	*gone*	*(the)*	*love's*	*happiness!*

ˈnɪm⇨ mɐ	kɔmt	iːᵃ	ˈvɔn⇨ nə ˈʃtʊndən
Nimmer	**kommt**	**ihr,**	**Wonnestunden,**
Never	*will return*	*you*	*blissful hours*

ˈmaɪ nəm	ˈhɛr tsən	meːᵃ	tsuː ˈrʏk
meinem	**Herzen**	**mehr**	**zurück.**
to my	*heart*	*anymore.*	¹⁾

ziː	ta ˈmiː no	ˈdiː zə	ˈtrɛː nən
Sieh,	**Tamino,**	**diese**	**Tränen**
Look,	*Tamino,*	*these*	*tears*

ˈfliː sən	ˈtraʊ tɐ	diːᵃ	ˈal⇨ laɪn
fließen,	**Trauter,**	**dir**	**allein.**
flow	*beloved*	*for you*	*alone.*

ˈfyːlst⇨	duː	ˈnɪçt⇨	deːᵃ	ˈliː bə	ˈzeː nən
Fühlst	**du**	**nicht**	**der**	**Liebe**	**Sehnen,**
Feel	*you*	*do not*	*(the)*	*love's*	*yearning,*

zoː	vɪrt⇨	ˈruː	ɪm	ˈtoː də	zaɪn
so	**wird**	**Ruh'**	**im**	**Tode**	**sein.**
then	*will*	*peace*	*in*	*death*	*be.*

¹⁾ Prefix to the verb "zurückkommen" (return)

THE INTERNATIONAL PHONETIC ALPHABET FOR ENGLISH

An overview of all the sounds found in American Standard (AS),
British Received (RP), and Mid-Atlantic (MA) Pronunciations.
by Kathryn LaBouff

CONSONANTS:

The following symbols are identical to the letters of our English (Roman) Alphabet:

[b], [d], [f], [g], [h], [k], [l], [m], [n], [p], [s], [t], [v], [w], [z]

The symbols below are NEW symbols added because no corresponding symbols exist in the Roman alphabet:

SYMBOL	KEY WORDS
[ŋ]	sing, think
[θ]	thin, thirst
[ð]	thine, this
[ʍ]	whisper, when
[j]	you, yes
[ʃ]	she, sure
[tʃ]	choose, church
[ʒ]	vision, azure
[dʒ]	George, joy
[ɹ]	red, remember, every (the burred r)
[R]	righteousness, great, realm (rolled r)
[ɾ]	very, far away, forever (flip r used between vowels)

VOWELS:

SYMBOL	KEY WORDS
[ɑ]	father, hot ("o" spellings in AS only)
[ɛ]	wed, many, bury
[ɪ]	hit, been, busy
[i]	me, chief, feat, receive
[ɨ]	pretty, lovely
[æ]	cat, marry, ask**, charity
[u]	too, wound, blue, juice
[ju]	view, beautiful, usual, tune
[ʊ]	book, bosom, cushion, full
[o]	obey, desolate, melody (unstressed syllables only)
[ɒ]	on, not, honest, God (RP & MA only)*
[ɔ]	awful, call, daughter, sought (AS)
[ɔ̹]	awful, call, daughter, sought (RP & MA)
[ɜ˞]	learn, burn, rehearse, journey (AS)
[ɜʳ]	learn, burn, rehearse, journey (RP & MA)
[ɚ]	father, doctor, vulgar, elixir (AS)
[əʳ]	father, doctor, vulgar, elixir (RP & MA)
[ʌ]	hum, blood, trouble, judge (stressed syllables)
[ə]	sofa, heaven, nation, joyous (unstressed syllables)

*The use of rolled and flipped R's and the short open o vowel are used in the British RP British and Mid-Atlantic dialect. They should not be used in American Standard dialect.

**[ɜ˞] and [ɚ] are the r colored vowels characteristic of American Standard Pronunciation, AS.
 [ɜʳ] and [əʳ] are the REDUCED r colored vowels found in British RP, and Mid-Atlantic, MA Pronunciations.

DIPHTHONGS:

SYMBOL	KEY WORDS
[aɪ]	n<u>igh</u>t, b<u>uy</u>, sk<u>y</u>
[eɪ]	d<u>ay</u>, br<u>ea</u>k, r<u>eig</u>n
[ɔɪ]	b<u>oy</u>, v<u>oi</u>ce, t<u>oi</u>l
[oʊ]	n<u>o</u>, sl<u>ow</u>, repr<u>oa</u>ch
[aʊ]	n<u>ow</u>, ab<u>ou</u>t, d<u>ou</u>bt
[ɛɚ]	<u>air</u>, c<u>are</u>, th<u>ere</u> (AS)
[ɛəʳ]	<u>air</u>, c<u>are</u>, th<u>ere</u> (RP & MA)
[ɪɚ]	<u>ear</u>, d<u>ear</u>, h<u>ere</u>, t<u>ier</u> (AS)
[ɪəʳ]	<u>ear</u>, d<u>ear</u>, h<u>ere</u>, t<u>ier</u> (RP & MA)
[ɔɚ]	p<u>our</u>, f<u>our</u>, s<u>oar</u>, o`<u>er</u> (AS)
[ɔəʳ]	p<u>our</u>, f<u>our</u>, s<u>oar</u>, o`<u>er</u> (RP & MA)
[ʊɚ]	s<u>ure</u>, t<u>our</u>, p<u>oor</u> (AS)
[ʊəʳ]	s<u>ure</u>, t<u>our</u>, p<u>oor</u> (RP & MA)
[ɑɚ]	<u>are</u>, h<u>ear</u>t, g<u>ar</u>den (AS)
[ɑəʳ]	<u>are</u>, h<u>ear</u>t, g<u>ar</u>den (RP & MA)

TRIPHTHONGS:

SYMBOL	KEY WORDS
[aɪɚ]	f<u>ire</u>, ch<u>oir</u>, adm<u>ire</u> (AS)
[aɪəʳ]	f<u>ire</u>, ch<u>oir</u>, adm<u>ire</u> (RP & MA)
[aʊɚ]	<u>our</u>, fl<u>ower</u>, t<u>ower</u> (AS)
[aʊəʳ]	<u>our</u>, fl<u>ower</u>, t<u>ower</u> (RP & MA)

ADDITIONAL SYMBOLS:

- [ˈ] A diacritical mark placed before a syllable that has primary stress.
- [ˌ] A diacritical mark placed before a syllable that has secondary stress.
- [ɾ] A flapped t or d. It is produced by flapping the tongue against the gum ridge. It is very characteristic of medial t's and d's in coloquial and southern American accents.
- [ʔ] A glottalized consonant, usually final or medial t's and d's. It is characteristic of conversational speech patterns in English. Ex: that day- thaʔ day   had done- haʔ done
- [(ʊ)] An off glide symbol. A weak extra vowel sounded after a primary vowel that is characteristic of certain Southern American accents.

GENERAL NOTES:

The texts in this guide have been transcribed into three primary pronunciations: American Standard, British Received and Mid-Atlantic Pronunciations. American Standard is a neutralized pronuncation of American English that is used for the American stage. British Received Pronunciation is an upper class pronunciation that is the performance standard for British works in the United Kingdom. Mid-Atlantic is a hybrid pronunciation that combines elements of both British and North American pronunciation. Some other variants found in this guide are for colloquial American or American Southern accents.

The standard performance practice for these arias was taken into consideration. The transcriptions were based on the character who sings them, the setting of the opera, and the geographic origin of the works. In general, if the composer and/or the text are North American, then the text is transcribed into American Standard pronunciation or one of the American variants. If the composer and or the text are British, then the text is transcribed into British Received Pronunciation. If the composer is North American but the text is British, then the text is transcribed into Mid-Atlantic. These are guidelines. The pronunciations can be modified to accommodate the production values of a specific operatic production or individual artistic taste.

THE BALLAD OF BABY DOE
music: Douglas Moore
libretto: John Latouche (based on the life of Baby Doe Tabor, 1854–1935)

Willow Song
In American Standard Pronunciation:

ˈwɪloʊ ʍɛɚ wi mɛt tʊˈgɛðɚ
Willow, where we met together,

ˈwɪloʊ ʍɛn aʊɚ lʌv wɑz nju
Willow, when our love was new.

ˈwɪloʊ ɪf hi wʌns ʃʊd bi ɹɪˈtɜ·nɪŋ
Willow, if he once should be returning,

pɹeɪ tɛl hɪm aɪ æm ˈwipɪŋ tu
Pray tell him I am weeping too.

soʊ fɑɚ fɹʌm ɪtʃ ˈʌðɚ
So far from each other,

ʍaɪl ðə deɪz pæs ɪn ðɛɚ ˈɛmptinɛs əˈweɪ
While the days pass in their emptiness away.

oʊ maɪ lʌv mʌst ɪt bi fɚˈɹɛvɚ
Oh my love, must it be forever,

ˈnɛvɚ wʌns əˈgɛn tu mit æz ɑn ðæʔ deɪ
Never once again to meet as on that day?

ænd ˈnɛvɚ ˌɹidɪsˈkʌvɚ ðə weɪ əv ˈtɛlɪŋ ðɛ weɪ əv ˈnoʊɪŋ
And never rediscover the way of telling, the way of knowing

ɔl aʊɚ hɑɚts wʊd seɪ
All our hearts would say?

gɔn ɑɚ ðə weɪz əv ˈplɛʒɚ
Gone are the ways of pleasure,

gɔn ɑɚ ðə fɹɛndz aɪ hæd əv jɔɚ
Gone are the friends I had of yore,

ˈoʊnli ðə ˌɹɛkəˈlɛkʃən ˈfeɪtəl
Only the recollection fatal

əv ðə wɜ·d ðæt wɑz ˈspoʊkən
Of the word that was spoken

ˈnɛvɚˈmɔɚ
Nevermore.

oʊ ˈwɪloʊ ʍɛɚ wi mɛt tʊˈgɛðɚ
Oh willow, where we met together,

ˈwɪloʊ ʍɛn aʊɚ lʌv wɑz nju
Willow, when our love was new.

ˈwɪloʊ ɪf hi wʌns ʃʊd bi ɹɪˈtɜ·nɪŋ
Willow, if he once should be returning,

pɹeɪ tɛl hɪm aɪ æm ˈwipɪŋ tu
Pray tell him I am weeping too.

Copyright © 1956 by Douglas S. Moore and John Latouche
Copyright Renewed
Chappell & Co., Owners of Publication and Allied Rights throughout the World.

The Silver Aria

In American Standard Pronunciation:

pliz ˈdʒɛntəlmən pliz
Please gentlemen, please,

goʊld ɪz ə faɪn θɪŋ fɔɚ ðoʊz hu ədˈmaɪɚ ɪt
Gold is a fine thing for those who admire it.

goʊld ɪz laɪk ðə sʌn
Gold is like the sun,

bʌt aɪ æm ə tʃaɪld əv ðə mun ænd ˈsɪlvɚ
But I am a child of the moon and silver.

ˈsɪlvɚ ɪz ðə ˈmɛtəl əv ðə mun
Silver is the metal of the moon,

ˈsikɹət ˈsmaɪlɚ ɹæpt ɪn ˈwʌndɚ
Secret smiler, wrapped in wonder,

floʊtɪŋ ɪn hɚ ˈklaʊdi ˈmædʒɪk
Floating in her cloudy magic,

tɪz ðə mun ðæt mɪnts hɚ ˈsɪlvɚ
T'is the moon that mints her silver

ɪn ðə dɪps əv ˈdɑɚkənd ɝθ
In the deeps of darkened earth.

ɔl ðæts ˈgloʊɪŋ kul ænd ˈtɛndɚ
All that's glowing, cool and tender,

hæz ðə fil əv ˈsɪlvɚ ɪn ɪt
has the feel of silver in it.

ˈsɪlvɚ ɪn æn ˈɪnfənts ˈlæftɚ
Silver in an infant's laughter,

ˈsɪlvɚ ɑn ðə ˈseɪdʒəz bɹaʊ
Silver on the sage's brow;

ˈsɪlvɚ ɪn ə ˈmunˈlɪt ˈɹɪvɚ
Silver in a moonlit river

ˈɛkoʊz ðə ˈsɪlvɚ ɔɚb əˈbʌv
echoes the silver orb above.

aɪ æm ə tʃaɪld əv ðə mun
I am a child of the moon

ænd ˈɔlweɪz wɪl əˈdɔɚ hɚ ˈɛləmənt
And always will adore her element.

ˈdɹimɪŋ æz aɪ wɑtʃ ɪt glim
Dreaming as I watch it gleam,

aɪ æm ˈmaɪnɪŋ ˈhɛvənli ɔɚ
I am mining heavenly ore.

goʊld ɪz ðə sʌn
Gold is the sun,

bʌt ˈsɪlvɚ laɪz ˈhɪdən ɪn ðə kɔɚ əv dɹimz
But silver lies hidden in the core of dreams

Copyright © 1956 by Douglas S. Moore and John Latouche
Copyright Renewed

Chappell & Co., Owners of Publication and
Allied Rights throughout the world

THE MEDIUM
music and libretto: Gian Carlo Menotti

The Black Swan
In American Standard Pronunciation:

ðə sʌn hæz ˈfɔlən ænd ɪt laɪz ɪn blʌd
The sun has fallen and it lies in blood.

ðə mun ɪz ˈwivɪŋ ˈbændədʒɪz əv goʊld
The moon is weaving bandages of gold.

oʊ blæk swɑn ʍɛɚ oʊ ʍɛɚ ɪz maɪ lʌvɚ gɔn
O black swan, where, oh, where, is my lover gone?

tɔːn ænd ˈtætɚd ɪz maɪ ˈbraɪdəl gaʊn
Torn and tattered is my bridal gown,

ænd maɪ læmp ɪz lɔst
And my lamp is lost.

wɪθ ˈsɪlvɚ ˈnidəlz ænd wɪθ ˈsɪlvɚ θɹɛd
With silver needles and with silver thread,

ðə stɑɚz stɪtʃ ə ʃraʊd fɔɚ ðə ˈdaɪŋ sʌn
The stars stitch a shroud for the dying sun.

oʊ blæk swɑn ʍɛɚ oʊ ʍɛɚ ɪz maɪ ˈlʌvɚ gɔn
O black swan, where, oh, where, is my lover gone?

aɪ hæd ˈgɪvən hɪm ə kɪs əv faɪɚ
I had given him a kiss of fire,

ænd ə ˈgoʊldən ɹɪŋ
And a golden ring.

ðoʊnt ju hɪɚ jɔɚ ˈlʌvɚ moʊn
Don't you hear your lover moan?

aɪz əv glæs ænd fit əv stoʊn
Eyes of glass and feet of stone,

ʃɛlz fɔɚ tiθ ænd widz fɔɚ tʌŋ
Shells for teeth and weeds for tongue,

ðip daʊn ɪn ðə ˈɹɪvɚz bɛd hɪz ˈlʊkɪŋ fɔɚ ðə ɹɪŋ
Deep down in the river's bed he's looking for the ring.

aɪz waɪd ˈoʊpən ˈnɛvɚ əˈslip
Eyes wide open, never asleep,

hiz ˈlʊkɪŋ fɔɚ ðə ɹɪŋ
he's looking for the ring.

ðə spulz ˈʌnˈɹævəl ænd ðə ˈnidəlz bɹeɪk
The spools unravel and the needles break.

ðə sʌn ɪz ˈbɛɹɪd ænd ðə stɑɚz wip
The sun is buried and the stars weep.

oʊ blæk weɪv teɪk mi əˈweɪ wɪð ju
O black wave, take me away with you.

aɪ	wɪl	ʃɛɚ	wɪð	ju	maɪ	ˈgoʊldən	hɛɚ
I	**will**	**share**	**with**	**you**	**my**	**golden**	**hair,**

ænd	maɪ	ˈbɹaɪdəl	kɹaʊn
and	**my**	**bridal**	**crown.**

oʊ	teɪk	mi	daʊn	wɪð	ju
Oh,	**take**	**me**	**down**	**with**	**you.**

teɪk	mi	daʊn	tu	maɪ	ˈwandɹɪŋ	lʌvɚ
Take	**me**	**down**	**to**	**my**	**wandr'ing**	**lover**

wɪð	maɪ	tʃaɪld	ˈʌnˈbɔɚn
with	**my**	**child**	**unborn.**

Copyright © 1947 by G. Schirmer, Inc. (ASCAP) New York, NY
International Copyright Secured. All Rights Reserved.

Monica's Waltz

In American Standard Pronunciation:

ˈbʀɹavoʊ ænd ˈæftɚ ðə ˈθiətɚ ˈsʌpɚ ænd dæns ˈmjuzɪk
Bravo! And after the theater, supper and dance. Music!

um pa pa um pa pa
Um- pa- pa, um- pa- pa,

ʌp ɪn ðə skaɪ ˈsʌmˈwʌn ɪz ˈpleɪɪŋ ə ˌtɹɑmˈboʊn ænd ə gɪˈtɑɚ
Up in the sky someone is playing a trombone and a guitar.

ɹɛd ɪz jɔɚ taɪ ænd ɪn jɔɚ ˌvɛlvɪˈtin koʊt ju haɪd ə stɑɚ
Red is your tie, and in your velvetine coat you hide a star.

ˈmɑnɪkə ˈmɑnɪkə dæns ðə wɔlts
Monica, Monica, dance the waltz,

ˈfɑloʊ mi mun ænd sʌn
Follow me, moon and sun,

kip taɪm wɪð mi wʌn tu θɹi wʌn
keep time with me, one two three one.

ɪf jʊɚ nɑt ʃaɪ pɪn ʌp maɪ hɛɚ wɪð jɔɚ stɑɚ
If you're not shy, pin up my hair with your star,

ænd ˈbʌkəl maɪ ʃu
and buckle my shoe.

ænd ʍɛn ju flaɪ pliz hoʊld ɑn taɪʔ tu maɪ weɪst
And when you fly, please hold on tight to my waist,

aɪm ˈflaɪɪŋ wɪð ju
I'm flying with you.

ˈmɑnɪkə ˈmɑnɪkə
Monica, Monica, etc.

ʍɑt ɪz ðə ˈmætɚ ˈtoʊbi
What is the matter Toby?

ʍɑt ɪz ɪʔ ju wɑnʔ tu tɛl mi
What is it you want to tell me?

nil daʊn bɪˈfɔɚ mi
Kneel down before me,

ænd naʊ tɛl mi
And now, tell me…

ˈmɑnɪkə ˈmɑnɪkə kænt ju si
Monica, Monica, can't you see,

ðæʔ maɪ hɑɚt ɪz ˈblidɪŋ ˈblidɪŋ fɔɚ ju
that my heart is bleeding, bleeding for you?

aɪ lʌvd ju ˈmɑnɪkə ɔl maɪ laɪf
I loved you, Monica, all my life,

wɪð ɔl maɪ bɹɛθ wɪð ɔl maɪ blʌd
with all my breath, with all my blood.

ju hɔnt ðə ˈmɪɹɚ əv maɪ slip ju ɑɚ maɪ naɪt
You haunt the mirror of my sleep, you are my night.

ju ɑɚ maɪ laɪt ænd ðə ˈdʒeɪlɚ əv maɪ deɪ
You are my light and the jailer of my day.

haʊ dɛɚ ju ˈskaʊndɹəl tɔk tu mi laɪk ðæt
How dare you, scoundrel, talk to me like that!

doʊnt ju noʊ hu aɪ æm
Don't you know who I am?

aɪm ðə kwin əv ˌɑ/æɹʊnˈdɛl
I'm the Queen of Aroundel!

aɪ ʃæl hæv ju pʊt ɪn tʃeɪnz
I shall have you put in chains!

ju ɑɚ maɪ ˈpɹɪnsɛs ju ɑɚ maɪ kwin
You are my princess, you are my queen,

ænd aɪm ˈoʊnli ˈtoʊbi wʌn əv jɔɚ sleɪvz
and I'm only Toby, one of your slaves,

ænd stɪl aɪ lʌv ju ænd ˈɔlweɪz lʌvd ju
And still I love you and always loved you

wɪð ɔl maɪ bɹɛθ wɪð ɔl maɪ blʌd
with all my breath, with all my blood.

aɪ lʌv jɔɚ ˈlæftɚ aɪ lʌv jɔɚ hɛɚ
I love your laughter, I love your hair,

aɪ lʌv jɔɚ dip ænd ˌnɑkˈtɝnəl aɪz
I love your deep and nocturnal eyes.

aɪ lʌv jɔɚ sɔft hændz soʊ ʍaɪt ænd wɪŋd
I love your soft hands, so white and winged,

aɪ lʌv ðə ˈslɛndɚ bɹæntʃ əv jɔɚ θɹoʊt
I love the slender branch of your throat.

ˈtoʊbi doʊn? spik tu mi laɪk ðæt
Toby, don't speak to me like that!

ju meɪk maɪ hɛd swɪm
You make my head swim.

ˈmɑnɪkə ˈmɑnɪkə foʊld mi ɪn jɔɚ ˈsætɪn gaʊn
Monica, Monica, fold me in your satin gown.

ˈmɑnɪkə ˈmɑnɪkə gɪv mi jɔɚ maʊθ
Monica, Monica, give me your mouth,

ˈmɑnɪkə ˈmɑnɪkə fɔl ɪn maɪ ɑɚmz
Monica, Monica, fall in my arms.

ʍaɪ	ˈtoʊbɪ	jʊɚ	nɑt	ˈkɹaɪɪŋ	ɑɚ	ju
Why,	**Toby!**	**You're**	**not**	**crying,**	**are**	**you?**

ˈtoʊbɪ	aɪ	wɑnt	ju	tu	noʊ
Toby,	**I**	**want**	**you**	**to**	**know**

ðæt	ju	hæv	ðə	moʊst	ˈbjutɪfʊl	vɔɪs	ɪn	ðə	wɝld
that	**you**	**have**	**the**	**most**	**beautiful**	**voice**	**in**	**the**	**world.**

Copyright © 1947 by G. Schirmer, Inc. (ASCAP) New York, NY
International Copyright Secured. All Rights Reserved.

TARTUFFE

music: Kirke Mechem
libretto: Kirke Mechem (after the play by Moliére)

Fair Robin I love

In Mid-Atlantic pronunciation:

ˈlɪsən ˌmæriˈæn
Listen, Mariane,

hɪəʳz æn oʊld sɔŋ
Here's an old song

əbaʊt ðæt kaɪnd ʌv mæn
About that kind of man,

ænd ʍɒʔ tu du ʍɛn hiz əˈweɪ
And what to do when he's away,

ɪts jɔəʳ ˈlɛsən fɔəʳ tuˈdeɪ
It's your lesson for today.

fɛəʳ Rˈ/ɹɒbɪn aɪ lʌv ænd ˈaʊəʳli aɪ daɪ
Fair Robin I love and hourly I die,

bʌt nɒt fɔr ə lɪp nɔr ə ˈlæŋgwɪʃɪŋ aɪ
But not for a lip, nor a languishing eye;

hiz ˈfɪkəl ænd fɔls ænd ðɛəʳ wi əˈgR/ɹi
He's fickle and false, and there we agree,

fɔəʳ a æm æz fɔls ænd æz ˈfɪkəl æz hi
For I am as false and as fickle as he.

wi ˈnaɪðəʳ bɪˈliv ʍɒt ˈaɪðəʳ kæn seɪ
We neither believe what either can say;

ænd ˈnaɪðəʳ bɪˈlivɪŋ wi ˈnaɪðəʳ bɪˈtR/ɹeɪ
And neither believing, we neither betray.

tɪz ˈsɪvəl tu swɛr ænd seɪ θɪŋz ʌv kɔəʳs
'Tis civil to swear and say things, of course;

wi min nɒt ðə ˈteɪkɪŋ fɔəʳ ˈbɛtəʳ ɔəʳ wɜʳs
We mean not the taking for better or worse.

ʍɛn ˈpR/ɹɛzənt wi lʌv ʍɛn ˈæbsənt əˈgR/ɹi
When present we love, when absent agree:

aɪ θɪŋk nɒt ʌv ˈR/ɹɒbɪn nɔəʳ ˈR/ɹɒbɪn ʌv mi
I think not of Robin, nor Robin of me.

ðə ˈlɛdʒənd ʌv lʌv noʊ ˈkʌpəl kæn faɪnd
The legend of love no couple can find,

soʊ ˈizɨ tu pɑəʳt ɔəʳ soʊ ˈizəli dʒɔɪnd
So easy to part or so easily joined.

Copyright © 1980 by G. Schirmer, Inc. (ASCAP) New York, NY
International Copyright Secured. All Rights Reserved.

G. SCHIRMER OPERA ANTHOLOGY

ARIAS FOR SOPRANO

Accompaniment CDs

On the recording:
William Billingham, piano

ACCOMPANIMENT CDS
CD TRACK LIST

CD ONE

THE BALLAD OF BABY DOE
1. Willow Song
2. The Silver Aria

UN BALLO IN MASCHERA
3. Saper vorreste

LA BOHÈME
4. Mi chiamano Mimì
5. Quando men vo
6. Donde lieta

CARMEN
7. Je dis que rien ne m'épouvante

LES CONTES D'HOFFMANN
8. Elle a fui, la tourterelle!

DON GIOVANNI
9. Batti, batti, o bel Masetto
10. Vedrai, carino

FALSTAFF
11. Sul fil d'un soffio etesio

FAUST
12. Ah! Je ris de me voir (The Jewel Song)

FIDELIO
13. O wär' ich schon mit dir vereint

DER FREISCHÜTZ
14. Kommt ein schlanker Bursch gegangen

GIANNI SCHICCHI
15. O mio babbino caro

GIULIO CESARE
16. V'adoro, pupille

ACCOMPANIMENT CDS
CD TRACK LIST

CD TWO

MADAMA BUTTERFLY
1. Un bel dì vedremo

MANON
2. Adieu, notre petite table

THE MEDIUM
3. The Black Swan
4. Monica's Waltz

LE NOZZE DI FIGARO
5. Porgi, amor
6. Dove sono i bei momenti
7. Deh vieni, non tardar

I PAGLIACCI
8. Stridono lassù

RIGOLETTO
9. Caro nome

ROMÉO ET JULIETTE
10. Ah! Je veux vivre

DER SCHAUSPIELDIREKTOR
11. Bester Jüngling

TARTUFFE
12. Fair Robin I love

TURANDOT
13. Signore, ascolta!
14. Tu che di gel sei cinta

DIE ZAUBERFLÖTE
15. Ach, ich fühl's

ABOUT THE PIANIST

WILLIAM BILLINGHAM

Pianist William Billingham is an assistant conductor at the Lyric Opera of Chicago, working with many of the world's leading opera singers and conductors. As a member of the music staff since 1995, Billingham has assisted in the preparation of over 70 productions, playing for rehearsals, coaching singers, conducting offstage musicians, and performing on piano, organ and harpsichord.

Billingham has also worked as a coach/accompanist for the Aspen Music Festival and School, the Cleveland Orchestra, the Florentine Opera (Milwaukee, WI), the Los Angeles Opera, and Lyric Opera of Chicago's Patrick G. and Shirley W. Ryan Opera Center. Active as a recital accompanist and chamber musician, he performs regularly with Midsummer's Music Festival in Door County, WI.

A native of Syracuse, NY, Billingham holds a Bachelor of Music degree in piano performance from the Oberlin Conservatory, a Master of Music in piano performance from the Peabody Conservatory, and a Doctor of Musical Arts in accompanying from the University of Southern California, where he studied with Gwendolyn Koldofsky and Brooks Smith. After brief teaching tenures at the University of Tennessee, Knoxville, and Ithaca College, he began his opera career in Germany as a repetitor at the opera houses in Heidelberg and Düsseldorf. He has recorded for Cedille Records and Hal Leonard Corporation.

ABOUT THE ENHANCED CDs

In addition to piano accompaniments playable on both your CD player and computer, these enhanced CDs also include tempo adjustment software for computer use only. This software, known as Amazing Slow Downer, was originally created for use in pop music to allow singers and players the freedom to independently adjust both tempo and pitch elements. Because we believe there may be valuable uses for these features in other musical genres, we have included this software as a tool for both the teacher and student. For quick and easy installation instructions of this software, please see below.

In recording a piano accompaniment we necessarily must choose one tempo. Our choice of tempo, phrasing, and dynamics is carefully considered. But by the nature of recording, it is only one option.

However, we encourage you to explore your own interpretive ideas, which may differ from our recordings. This software feature allows you to adjust the tempo up and down without affecting the pitch. We recommend that this tempo adjustment feature be used with care and insight.

The audio quality may be somewhat compromised when played through the Amazing Slow Downer. This compromise in quality will not be a factor in playing the CD audio track on a normal CD player or through another audio computer program.

INSTALLATION FROM DOWNLOAD:

For Windows (XP, Vista or 7):
1. Download and save the .zip file to your hard drive.
2. Extract the .zip file.
3. Open the "ASD Lite" folder.
4. Double-click "setup.exe" to run the installer and follow the on-screen instructions.

For Macintosh (OSX 10.4 and up):
1. Download and save the .dmg file to your hard drive.
2. Double-click the .dmg file to mount the "ASD Lite" volume.
3. Double-click the "ASD Lite" volume to see its contents.
4. Drag the "ASD Lite" application into the Application folder.

INSTALLATION FROM CD:

For Windows (XP, Vista or 7):
1. Load the CD-ROM into your CD-ROM drive.
2. Open your CD-ROM drive. You should see a folder named "Amazing Slow Downer." If you only see a list of tracks, you are looking at the audio portion of the disk and most likely do not have a multi-session capable CD-ROM.
3. Open the "Amazing Slow Downer" folder.
4. Double-click "setup.exe" to install the software from the CD-ROM to your hard disk. Follow the on-screen instructions to complete installation.
5. Go to "Start," "Programs" and find the "Amazing Slow Downer Lite" application. Note: To guarantee access to the CD-ROM drive, the user should be logged in as the "Administrator."

For Macintosh (OSX 10.4 or higher):
1. Load the CD-ROM into your CD-ROM drive.
2. Double-click on the data portion of the CD-ROM (which will have the Hal Leonard icon in red and be named as the book).
3. Open the "Amazing OS X" folder.
4. Double-click the "ASD Lite" application icon to run the software from the CD-ROM, or copy this file to your hard drive and run it from there.

MINIMUM SOFTWARE REQUIREMENTS:

For Windows (XP, Vista or 7):
Pentium Processor; Windows XP, Vista, or 7; 8 MB Application RAM; 8x Multi-Session CD-ROM drive

For Macintosh (OS X 10.4 or higher):
Power Macintosh or Intel Processor; Mac OS X 10.4 or higher; MB Application RAM; 8x Multi-Session CD-ROM drive